ASTERING BLUES KEYBOARD

Alfred, the leader in educational publishing, and the National Keyboard Workshop, one of America's finest contemporary music schools, have joined forces to bring you the best, most progressive educational tools possible. We hope you will enjoy this book and encourage you to look for other fine products from Alfred and the National Keyboard Workshop.

This book was acquired, edited and produced by Workshop Arts, Inc., the publishing arm of the National Guitar Workshop.
Nathaniel Gunod, editor
Joe Bouchard, music typesetter
Cathy Bolduc, design
CD recorded at Bar None Studios, Cheshire, CT
Cover photograph: Karen Miller

TABLE OF CONTENTS

ABOUT THE AUTHOR

Merrill Clark attended the University of Utah as a jazz theory major on full scholarship, where he studied with Dr. William Fowler and film composer Pat Williams. He graduated *Magna cum Laude* in 1978. His compositions have been performed throughout the country. He has been awarded many honors including being named "Outstanding Composer" at the 1972 American College Jazz Festival. He has been composing, performing and teaching in New York City since 1979. From 1983 to 1988, he was Director of Jazz Studies at SOJ Studios where he taught workshops, composed, arranged and recorded on keyboards, bass and guitar. In 1985, he was awarded a grant from "Meet the Composer" to present a concert of original compositions featuring jazz violinist, John Blake, Jr. Recent major compositions include a one-act opera, *Sanctuary for Two Violins Under Assault* (commissioned by Joseph Papp), a quadruple fugue for chamber orchestra entitled *Melee*, a ballet for electric viola d'amore and percussion, *The Tragedy of Tarpeia*, and a two-act opera based on Oscar Wilde's *The Picture of Dorian Gray*. Merrill is currently a solfegist on the staff at A.S.C.A.P. (The American Society of Composers, Authors and Publishers).

INTRODUCTION

Welcome to *Mastering Blues Keyboard.* If you have completed *Beginning Blues Keyboard* and *Intermediate Blues Keyboard*, the first two books of this method, you should have a solo repertoire representing many styles to perform and improvise on.

To get the most out of this book, you should also:

- Be able to function in a variety of ensemble formats from duos with guitarists, bassists or vocalists to being part of a complete rhythm section.
- Have at your fingertips a sizeable basic blues vocabulary of classic phrases, chord progressions, turnarounds and bass lines, as well as styles and feels.
- Be familiar with the general outline of the historical development of the blues.
- Know about some of the major figures from each period and geographical area. Hopefully, you have begun to collect recordings by the artists mentioned thus far and are spending quality time listening to them.

In this book, there will be more information of a theoretical nature. It's up to you to take each idea and find a personal way to use it. Most of the examples in this book are written in the key of C for convenience, but they should be played in all keys. For the more difficult pieces and passages, it is a good idea to learn the hands separately before combining them. Practice with a metronome. Start the study of each piece or figure slowly enough so that you can play it without mistakes. Increase the tempo gradually and, when a piece is fast enough, use the click as a back beat (on two and four of the bar only). When you play a note precisely on the click, the click will not be heard.

Playing the blues well is a lifetime pursuit. The three books of this method are just a starting point. Remain open to new possibilities and information while always maintaining your connection with the roots of the blues—the core body of skills and historical continuity that make the blues what it is. Above all, I hope that you will find this material useful, and that you will enjoy your studies.

A compact disc is available for this book. This disc can make learning with this book easier and more enjoyable. This symbol will appear next to every example that is on the CD. Use the CD to help insure that you are capturing the feel of the examples, interpreting the rhythms correctly, and so on. The track numbers below the symbols correspond directly to the example you want to hear. Track 1 will help you tune your electronic keyboard to the CD. Have fun!

ACKNOWLEDGEMENTS

Thanks to everyone at the National Keyboard Workshop, Nat Gunod and Joe Bouchard in particular. Thanks also to: Alan Weight; Bob Gibson; Dan Waldis; Dr. William Fowler; Ladd McIntosh; John Blake, Jr.; John Castellano; Pat Williams; Ramiro Cortes; Dr. Joyce Newman; Neal Haiduck; Steve Lynch; Richard Fairfax; Tricia Woods; Samir Chatterjee; Louis Bauzo; Steve Turre and Akua Dixon-Turre; Joe Covey; Brenda Vincent; Taleatia Shannon Vincent-Clark; all my students over the years (who completed my education); every musician I ever listened to or transcribed (I never heard anyone from whom I didn't learn something); and special thanks to Albert Bouchard, Deborah Frost and Ace.

CHAPTER 1

Review

TRIADS

A chord is a structure built from three or more notes. The most basic type of chord is a triad, a three note chord. A triad is built with a root (1), 3rd (3) and 5th (5). We learned four types of triads.

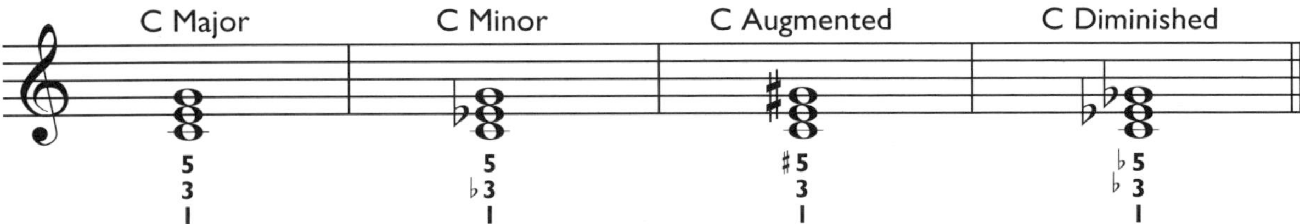

Any triad can be inverted.

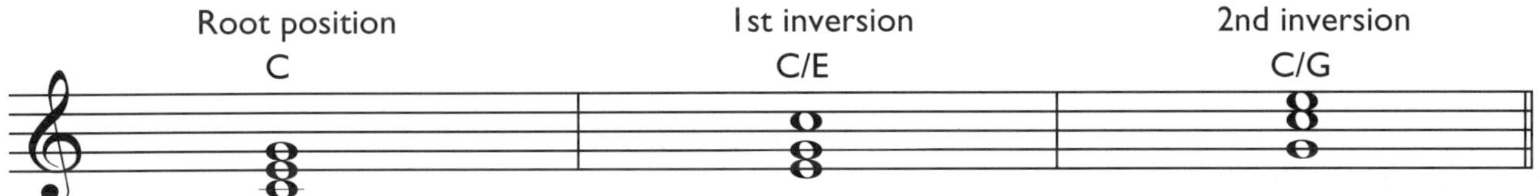

DOMINANT 7TH CHORDS

Let's look at the notes of the major scale and notice every other note:

C	D	**E**	F	**G**	A	**B**
1	2	**3**	4	**5**	6	**7**

We can use every other note of the scale to build a four-note chord:

C	E	G	B	
1	3	5	7	This is a **C Major 7** chord.

To make a C Dominant 7th chord, or **C7**, we lower the 7th by a half step (♭7), from B to B♭.

C	E	G	B♭	
1	3	5	♭7	This is a **C7** chord.

You also need to be able to easily invert dominant 7th chords.

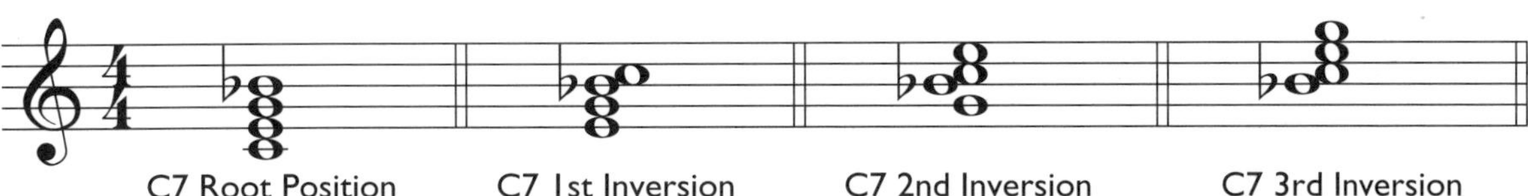

Something to notice: with the exception of root position, you always have a whole step between the dominant 7th and the root in your voicing.

EXTENSIONS

So far, we have been looking at chords with four or less different notes. We can add more notes to our chords. The extra notes are called *extensions*. Extensions on a chord do not change the chord's function, but they do change its color.

Remember, we build chords in 3rds (using every other note of a scale). Following the 7th, the next chord tone is the 9th. The chart below shows the chord tones and the extensions beyond the 7th. For convenience, we'll relate it to a C root.

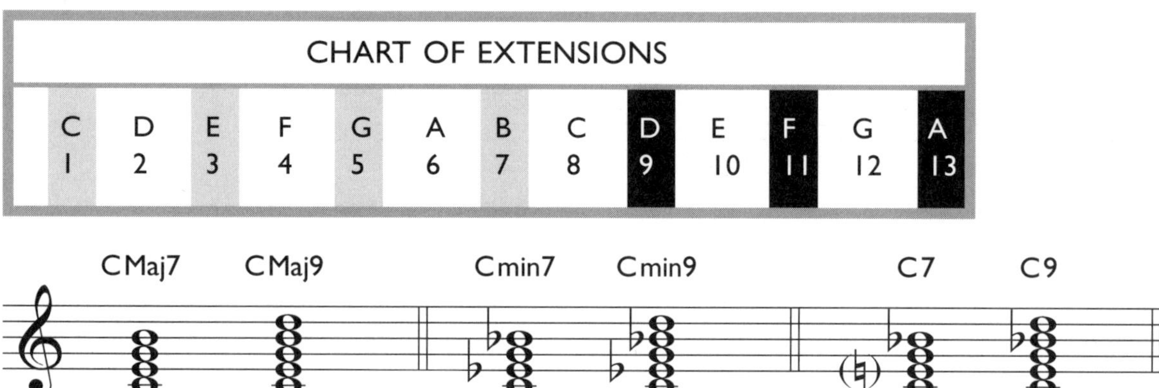

CHART OF EXTENSIONS

C	D	E	F	G	A	B	C	D	E	F	G	A
1	2	3	4	5	6	7	8	9	10	11	12	13

= Chord tones

= Extensions

Notice that the extensions are simply the notes of the scale in the next octave. For example, the 9th is the 2nd in the next octave. Extensions give us more possibilities for voice leading because we have more notes from which to choose. We must use extensions with care, however, or they will detract from, rather than add something to, the music. Blues keyboardists frequently use 9ths as the top voice of their chords. We'll look at an example of this shortly.

Continuing up the scale past the 9th, we reach the 11th and the 13th. These are common extensions but they are not all used on all types of chords. The 11th, for instance, doesn't sound good on a major or dominant 7th chord because it clashes with the major 3rd (it is, after all, just the 4th up one octave). It sounds fine, however, on a minor chord. The 13th is used most frequently on dominant 7th chords.

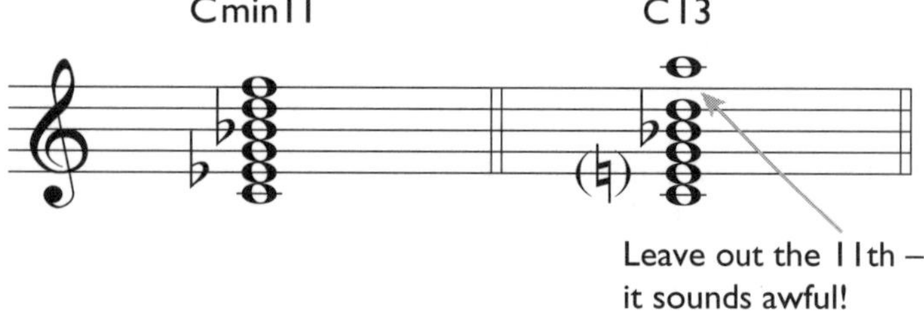

On dominant chords, extensions may be altered by raising or lowering them a half step. The way we notate a chord with an altered extension in this book is to list the altered extension separately from the rest of the chord, placing a comma before it. Extensions are always listed from the lowest to the highest.

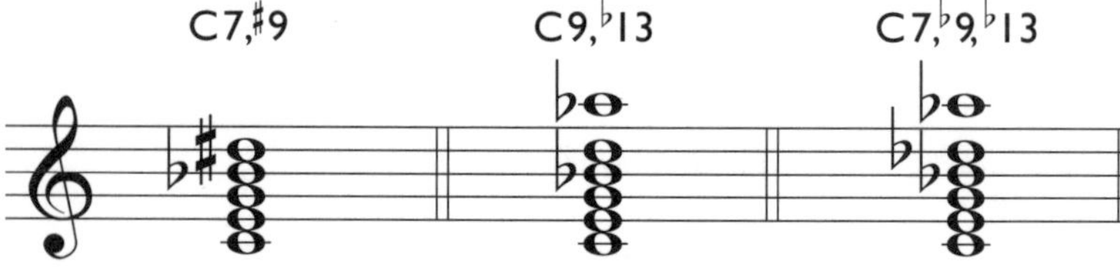

OPEN VOICINGS AND DOUBLINGS

Below is an eight-bar blues arranged with open voicings. With the exception of the first, fourth and fifth measures, each measure is voiced with a dominant 7th chord. Since dominant 7th chords have four notes (R, 3rd, 5th, ♭7th), we might expect to play two of those notes in one hand and the remaining two in the other. Generally, this is how open voicings work. There are, however, always exceptions.

Some chords have more notes than can be played at once, so we must choose what notes to leave out. With smaller chords, like triads, we may want to add notes, and so must choose what to double. Including the 5th in a chord voicing doesn't necessarily add to the sound, so we sometimes leave it out. In the first chord of bar 7 of this example, the 5th is omitted and the root is doubled. The 3rd and 7th are generally not doubled (unless one of them is the melody note). Doubling 3rds and 7ths makes things sound too muddy!

Notice that the first chord, C, is voiced as a triad rather than a dominant 7th. This is characteristic of an eight bar blues; the sound of the dominant chord is emphasized in bar 2, setting up the move to the IV chord in bar 3. The I to IV can sound like V to I.

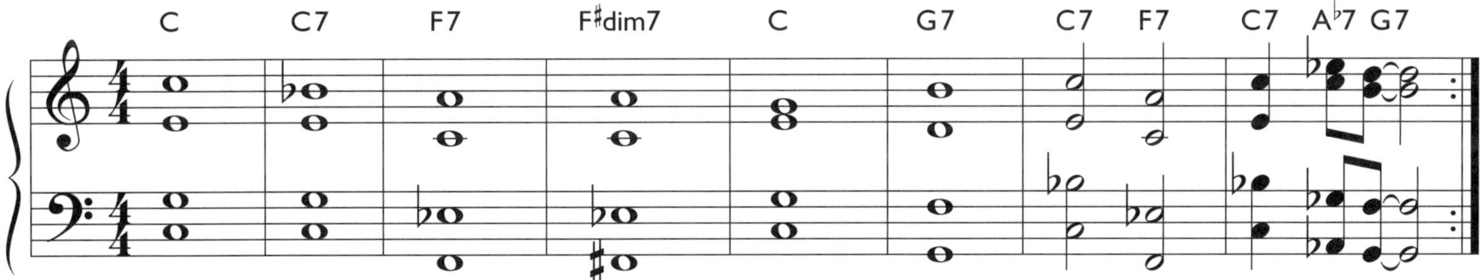

SHELL VOICINGS

Since the perfect 5th is present in Maj7, 7 and min7 chords, we don't need it to define the sound of the chord. Therefore, we can play these economical voicings with the roots in the left hand and the 3rd and 7th in the right hand. When the roots move down in 5ths (or up in 4ths), the voice leading in the right hand is very smooth.

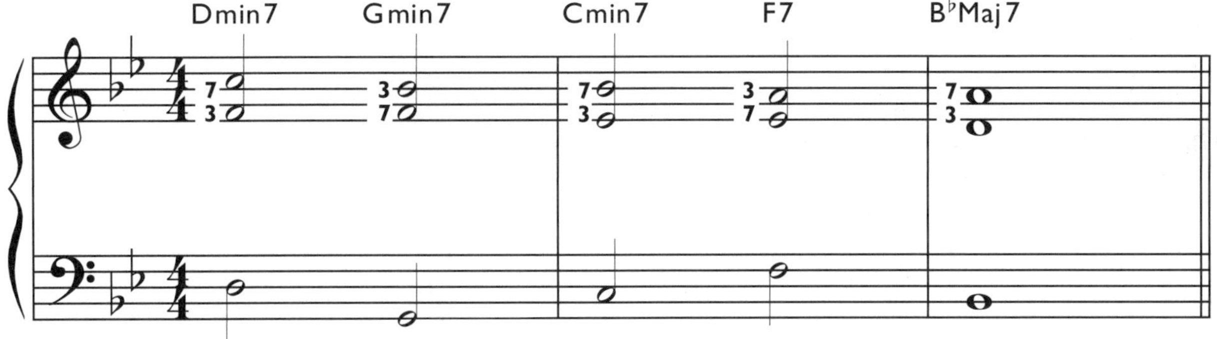

ROOTS, 3RDS, 7THS AND 10THS

In most cases, the root, 3rd and 7th of a chord define a chord's function and quality. In some blues styles, you can play solely a combination of roots, 3rds and 7ths for your left-hand accompaniment. It's necessary to be very familiar with the locations of the 3rds and 7ths in every key so you can use them easily for your blues progressions.

If you are playing with a bass player, you can play just the 3rd and 7th of each chord.

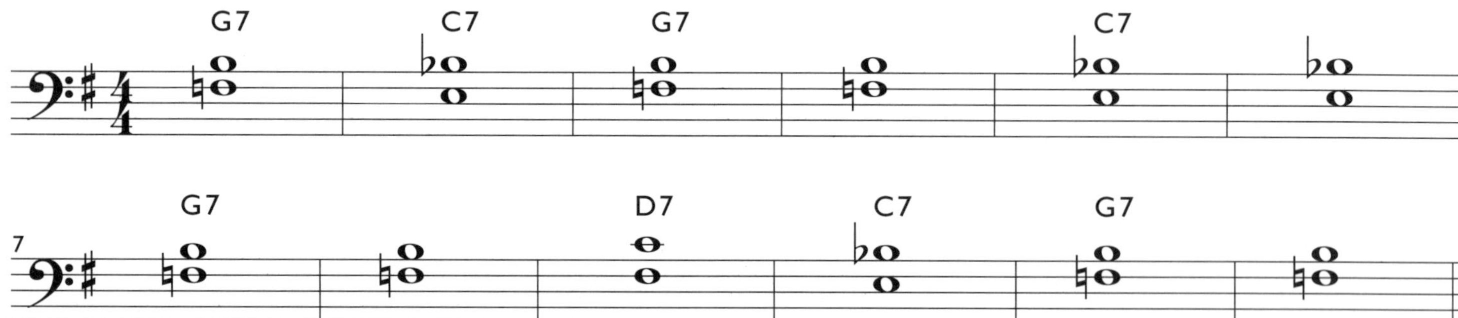

When playing solo, alternate between the root-7th and root-3rd.

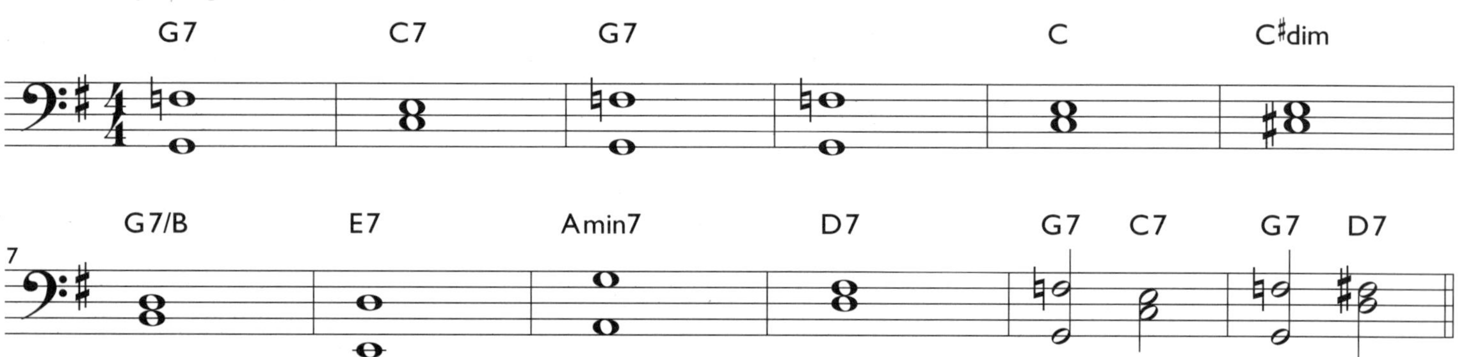

If your hand is big enough, you can play 10ths, one of the nicest sounds on the piano. A 10th is simply a 3rd with an extra octave inserted, giving it a more open sound. If you can't reach a 10th, fake it by rolling your hand quickly from the bottom note to the top note.

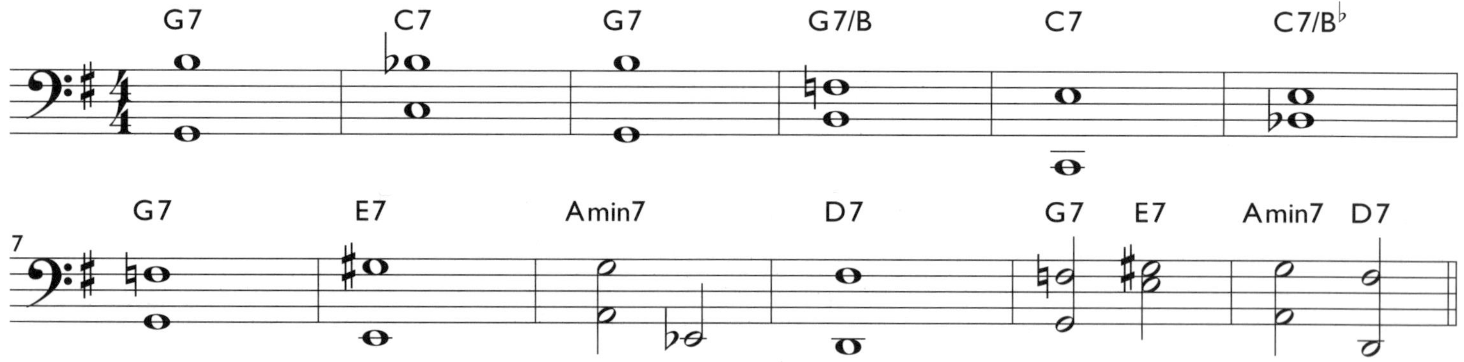

For a fuller sound, combine some walking lines with 3rds, 7ths and 10ths.

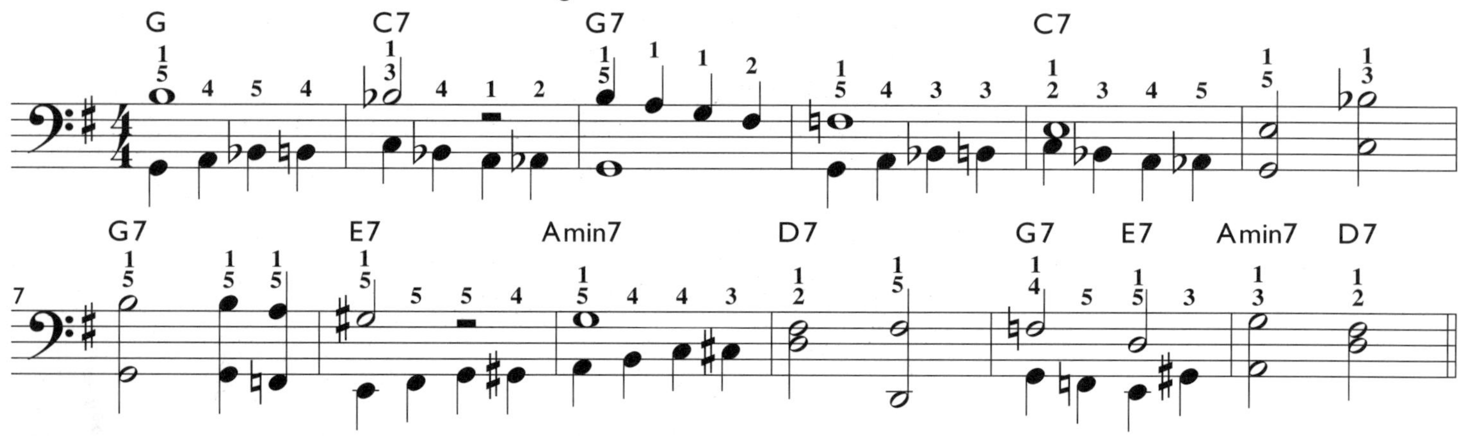

SWING FEEL

The blues often has a $\frac{12}{8}$ feel. The time signature is still $\frac{4}{4}$, but we take each quarter note and divide it into three. In other words, we play *eighth-note triplets.* Instead of playing two eighth notes per beat, we play three. Each bar then contains twelve triplet eighth-notes, which is why it is called $\frac{12}{8}$ feel, or triplet feel. It is also called *shuffle* feel.

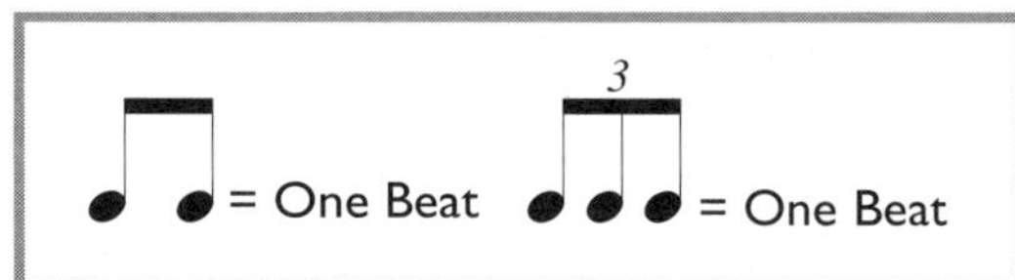

Let's get used to this feel by staying on the I chord, C Major, and playing eighth-note triplets with your right hand. Set your metronome to about 70 beats per minute and play three triplet eighth-notes on each click.

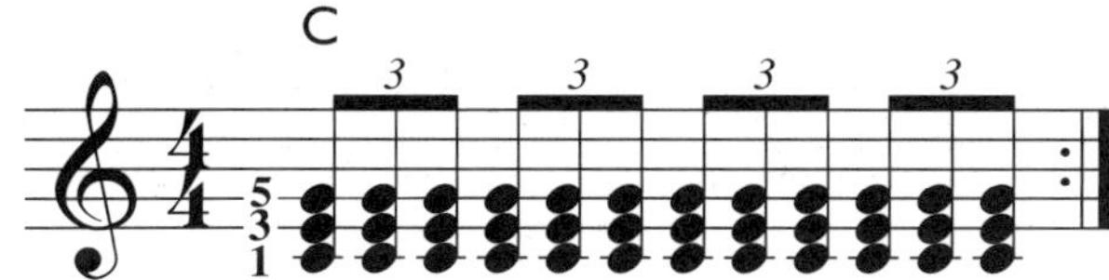

In this book, everything should be played with a swing feel unless marked "*Straight 8ths.*"

In a typical shuffle bass pattern, we play triplets in the right hand. We also use the triplet feel in the left hand, but instead of writing triplets we write eighth notes with an indication that the eighths are *swung. Swinging the eighths* means that the first eighth note of each beat is held longer than the second.

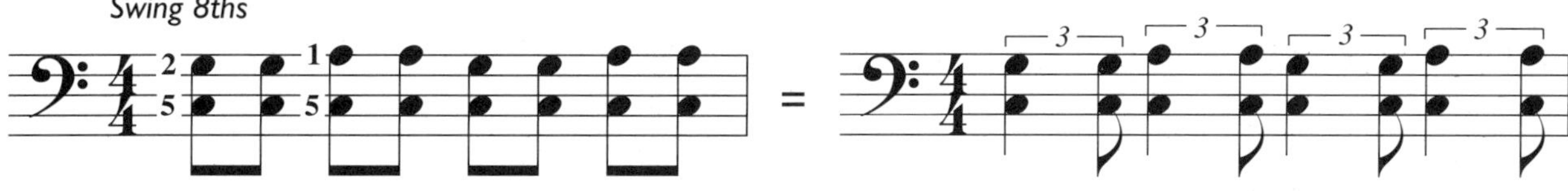

CYCLE OF 5THS

If we move from key to key at an interval of a perfect 5th, a sharp or flat will be added to the key signature each time we move. This movement is known as the *cycle of 5ths* (sometimes called the *circle* of 5ths). The cycle of 5ths forms the basis for most harmonic movement in popular music.

Since an inverted perfect 5th is a perfect 4th, the cycle of 5ths is sometimes called the cycle of 4ths. It's the same thing. Usually, when blues players think "cycle of 5ths," they are thinking counterclockwise through the cycle—down by 5ths: C, F, B♭, E♭, etc.

The major key cycle is on the inside. The relative minor for each major key is outside the circle. Just like the major keys, the minor keys move up in 5ths as you add sharps, and down in 5ths as you add flats to the key signature.

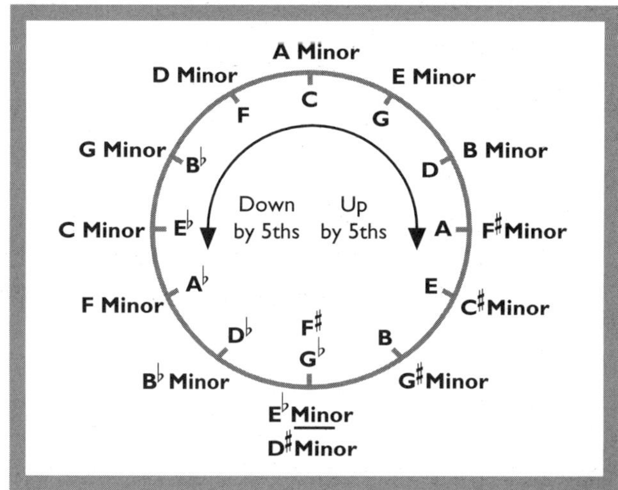

REVIEW OF RHYTHMIC FEELS

Let's review some different grooves. The definition of each feel will include the rhythmic fundamentals and a description of a typical bass part. Good keyboard parts are a result of complementing and accentuating these two things (or for solo piano, covering all three).

SHUFFLE

Your old friend the shuffle is marked by a strong triplet feel and a strong *backbeat*, which means the second and fourth beats of each bar are emphasized in the drum part. Shuffle bass patterns typically outline the chord, using a swing eighth rhythm.

SWING

The eighth notes in a swing feel are swung, but the triplet feel is not necessarily emphasized. The main emphasis is on the quarter note—four beats per bar played on the ride cymball The backbeat is present (the drummer plays the high-hat on 2 and 4) but not heavily emphasized. The bass generally walks:

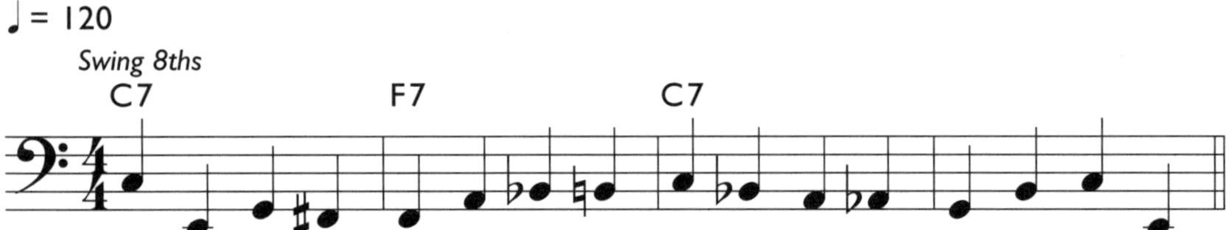

SLOW $\frac{12}{8}$

Slow $\frac{12}{8}$ time is often written in $\frac{4}{4}$ and marked "triplet feel." Combine a triplet feel with a walking bass line and decrease the tempo as for a slow blues. The drummer emphasizes the quarter note and the triplet feel simultaneously.

THE TWO FEEL

A variation on swing. Instead of marking every quarter note, just 1 and 3 are emphasized (sounding like two beats per measure). Up-tempo swing tunes sometimes start out in a two feel. The bass plays simply—mainly on beats 1 and 3, alternating roots and chord tones.

SECOND-LINE GROOVE

Second line is the name given a rhythm the drummers in the second line of a New Orleans funeral procession played. The eighth-note feel is somewhere between straight and swung. The backbone of second-line groove is this dotted-quarter note pattern:

Bass parts for second-line grooves are based on the same pattern:

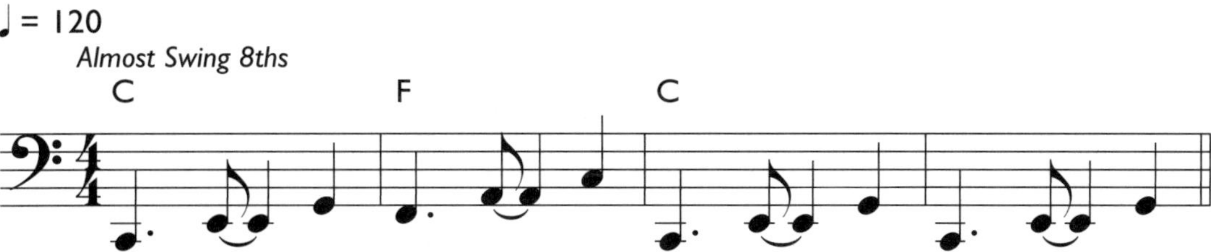

FUNK

The basic elements of funk grooves are straight eighths, a strong feeling of four and sixteenth note creativity. Having your sixteenth note rhythms together is an important part of being a competent modern blues and R&B player.

RHUMBA

Afro-Cuban in origin, rhumba inspired rhythms have been incorporated into both blues and jazz. The feel is similar to a second-line groove but the eighth notes are completely straight.

WALKING BASS LINES

Once you understand the fundamentals of building a walking bass line (Chapter 9, page 90, *Beginning Blues Keyboard*) the next step is to develop your vocabulary. Knowing that there is more than one way to get from the I chord to the IV chord is one thing, but having it under your fingers is another. You need to practice different ways of getting through chord progressions so you don't always play exactly the same thing. As always, the best way to discover new sounds is by listening to recordings and transcribing what you hear. Here are some typical walking patterns to get you started.

SIX WAYS TO GET TO THE IV CHORD ON THE DOWNBEAT OF BAR 2

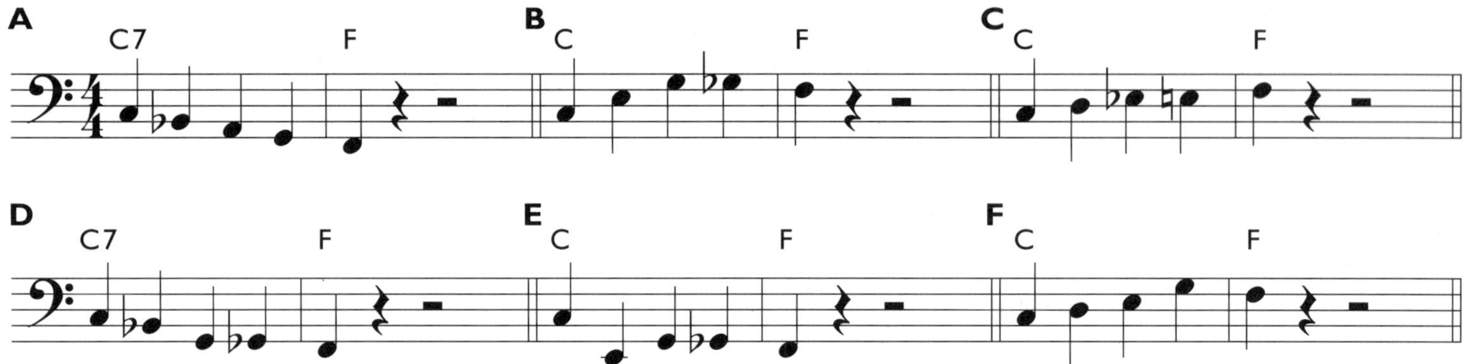

FOUR ROUTES BACK TO I

These assume that we used example A above to get to the IV chord.

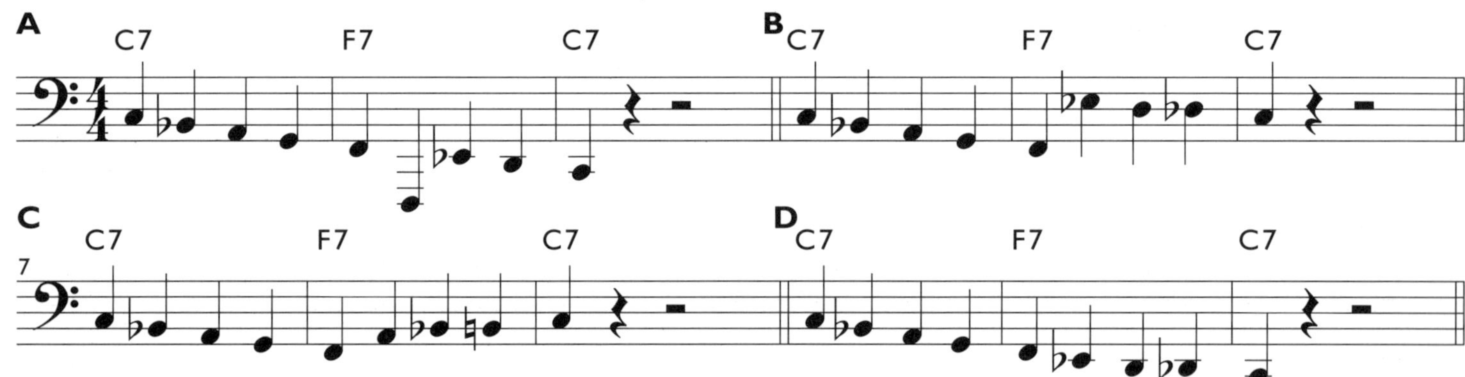

FOUR WAYS TO STAY ON I FOR EIGHT BEATS

Sometimes it seems tricky to stay on one chord for several bars. Each of these two-bar ideas can be repeated to fill four bars.

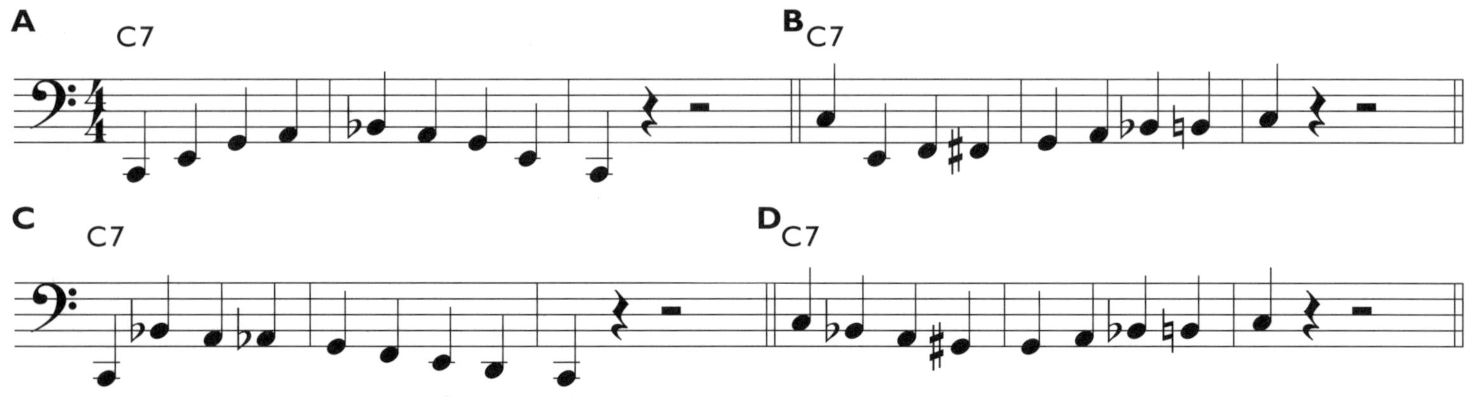

FOUR WAYS TO WALK THROUGH I-vi-ii-V

In Chapter 2 of *Intermediate Blues Keyboard*, you played an eight-bar blues called *Foolish Blues*. Here are two choruses of walking through the same blues progression. If you can recall the melody you learned, add it in your right hand.

Top Ten Tips for Walking Bass Lines

1. Play the root on beat one of the bar frequently. The 5th can work, too, or in the proper context, another chord tone such as the ♭7.
2. Think ahead—know where you are going.
3. Play primarily diatonic tones on the strong beats of the bar (beats 1 and 3). Reserve leading tones, passing tones or chromatic tones for the weak beats (beats 2 and 4).
4. Repeat notes (especially the root) if you wish.
5. Add occasional eighth notes if they make the line flow more smoothly.
6. Combine measures of walking with other typical bass patterns (boogie, shuffle, etc.).
7. Think of the bass line as a second melody.
8. Sing a bass line, then play it.
9. Vary your lines with octaves.
10. Keep it simple.

TREMOLOS AND OTHER BLUES SOUNDS

TREMOLOS

You've heard them—maybe you've already played them. If you haven't, you undoubtedly want to. *Tremolos* in the right hand, over a nice shuffle groove, are an essential ingredient in the blues sound. A tremolo is a rapid alternation between two notes. Sometimes blues players will call this a *roll.*

You can tremolo or roll between the root and the ♭3 of the key over almost the whole blues progression.

This is how tremolos or rolled notes are notated in the written music:

Tremolo on F and A♭ for five beats.

Tremolos are sometimes indicated like this:

CLUSTERS

A *cluster* is a group of notes that do not belong together as a chord but are played simultaneously. Often, it's just one of the notes that doesn't fit with the others. Below is an excerpt from a piece in the style of Otis Spann that was presented on page 49 of *Beginning Blues Keyboards*. The cluster (A♯, B, D) is hit as a chord and then arpeggiated.

GRACE NOTES/CRUSH TONES

When we play these figures off of triads, it's nice to add the ♭3 as a *grace note* preceeding the 3rd. A grace note is a quick ornamental note played directly before the main note. It is sometimes called a crush tone. Some of us call this *bending the 3rd* because it sounds similar to a guitar player bending a note. It feels more natural in some keys than in others, depending upon where the black notes and white notes fall under your fingers. Here's how it works:

If the ♭3 is a black note, and the 3 is a white note, as in the keys of C, F or G, you can simply slide your 2nd finger from the ♭3 to the 3.

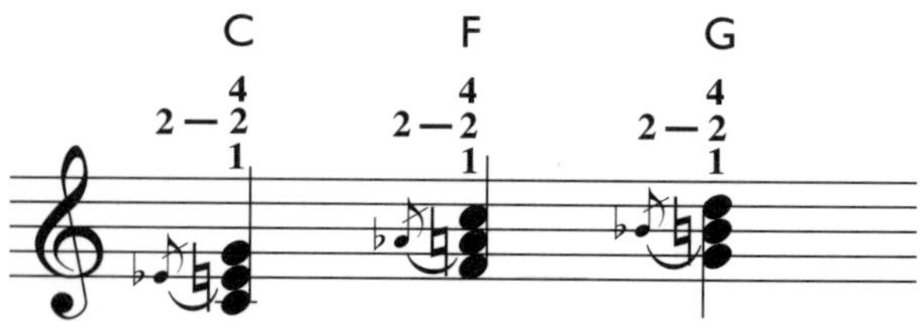

If the ♭3 is a white note, and the 3 is a black note, it's a little more awkward. Try playing the ♭3 with your 2nd finger and the 3 with your 3rd finger.

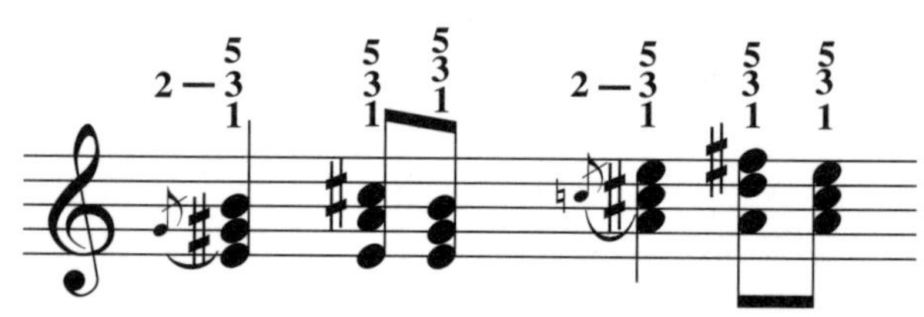

THE BASIC FORMS

TWELVE BARS

The classic twelve-bar blues form is as follows:

I	I	I	I	IV	IV	I	I	V	IV	I	I
1	2	3	4	5	6	7	8	9	10	11	12

A "quick four" in bar 2 is common, as is a half cadence (to V) in bar 12.

I	IV	I	I	IV	IV	I	I	V	IV	I	V
1	2	3	4	5	6	7	8	9	10	11	12

EIGHT BARS

Here are two common eight-bar progressions:

#1

I	i7	IV7	♯ivdim	I	V7	I	V7
1	2	3	4	5	6	7	8

#2

I	I7	IV7	♭VII	I vi	ii V	I vi	ii V
1	2	3	4	5	6	7	8

SIXTEEN BARS

The classic sixteen-bar form appeared in Herbie Hancock's *Watermelon Man.*

I7	I7	I7	I7	IV7	IV7	I7	I7
1	2	3	4	5	6	7	8

V7	IV7	V7	IV7	V7	IV7 break	I7	I7
9	10	11	12	13	14	15	16

Another common sixteen-bar form has eight bars of I7, usually in stop-time or stop-time with a riff, followed by the last eight bars of a standard twelve-bar blues.

TURNAROUNDS

A *turnaround* is a musical figure used to lead you back to the top of the form. A turnaround usually ends on a V7 chord (a *half cadence*) since the dominant V7 chord leads back to the tonic.

BASIC TURNAROUNDS

Bass walks up from the 3rd of the I chord to the root of the V chord.

Bass walks down from the ♭7 of the I chord to the root of the V chord.

We can put these two *chromatic* (using notes outside the key) approaches together with two hands.

The word "chromatic" also implies movement in half-step increments, as in the *chromatic scale* (a twelve-note scale which includes all of the white notes and all of the black notes on the piano).

NEIGHBORING CHORDS

To play more involved turnarounds, you need to be familiar with the neighboring chords for the key. Neighboring chords lie a half step away from the chord you are approaching. A♭7 is a neighboring chord to G7. D♭7 is a neighboring chord to C7.

Here is a basic turnaround with a neighboring chord used to approach the V chord:

ENDINGS AND INTROS

Endings have the opposite function of turnarounds. Instead of taking us back to the top of the form, they take us out. Interestingly, you can transform many turnaround figures into endings just by ending on a I chord instead of the V7.

Here's a familiar turnaround transformed into an ending:

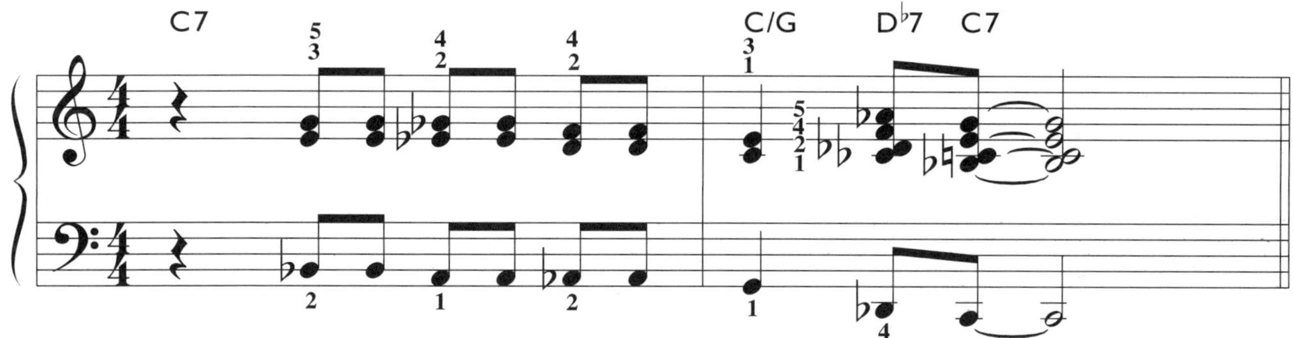

This ending approaches the I chord from below:

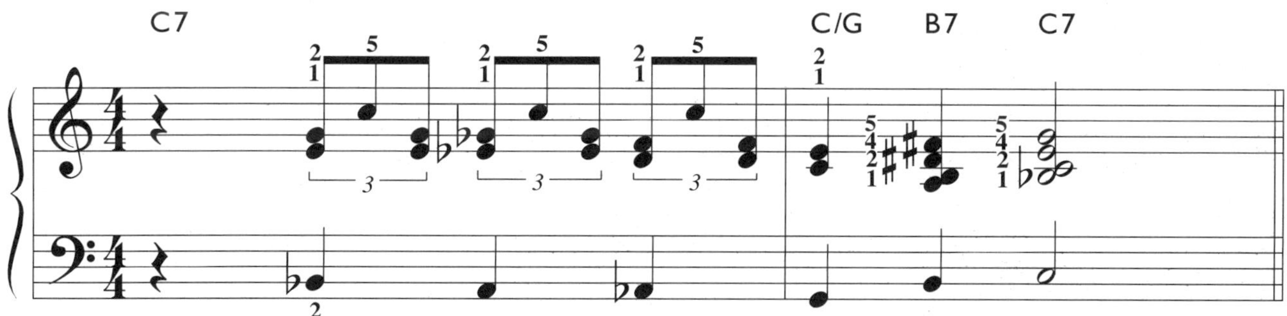

Not every blues starts with an introduction, but many of them do. As with every other aspect of the blues that we've talked about, there is some standard vocabulary to learn, as well as some room for creativity.

A common way to start a blues is to play a four-bar, V-IV-I intro with a little turnaround at the end.

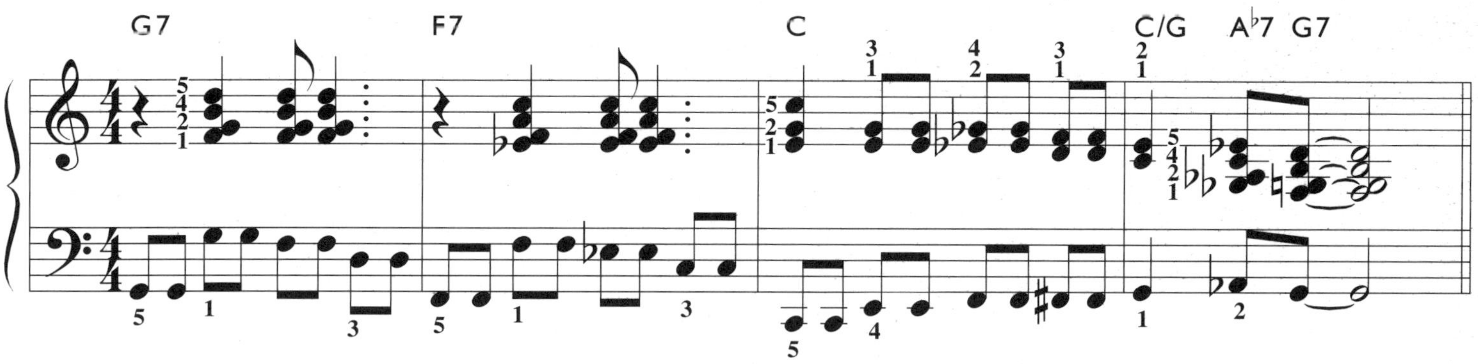

CHAPTER 2

Improvising and Soloing

MOTIFS

Let's investigate what makes a musical line become an "old friend" that you're happy to hear every time you put on a CD. It's almost mystical, but the use of *motifs* (short rhythmic or melodic figures that recur) has a lot to do with it.

Every chorus of blues that you play should be unique. There are two ways to achieve this:

1) **Archival**. Many fine improvisers have learned hundreds of motifs from past masters which they use at appropriate moments.
2) **Spontaneous**. Creating new motifs.

This chapter will deal with spontaneous musical invention. Here are some ideas to help you make motifs that may qualify:

VERBAL

Remember, blues is lyric-based music. Use the rhythm, inflection and structure of language as a source for motifs. For instance, the phrase *"Don't you give me no lip!"* can give us this rhythm:

> In this book, everything should be played with a swing feel unless marked "*Straight 8ths.*"

The inflection may change depending on which word you want to emphasize. High notes or low notes both provide accentuation. Here's a way that idea can be applied to our motif:

Structure comes when the line is inserted into verse form. We need to bear in mind that vocalists improvise with text using interjections, repetitions and new ideas.

NON-VERBAL

Motivic material can also be created non-verbally using patterns, numeric manipulation (for instance, using scale degrees based on a telephone number) and inspiration.

Collect motifs that you like in a manuscript notebook.

DEVELOPING A MOTIF

Once you have a motif, it's only a germ from which a melody can grow. Now we need to use it to tell a story. It must be developed. Here are some ideas to use:

The recommended tempo for all the examples on this page is ♩ = 104.

REPEAT

There are two good reasons for this: 1) so the listener will remember it; and 2), to give your solo shape. The **"golden rule of repetition"** has been used by all the greats, from Bach to Bo Diddley. The rule is the basis of the blues form: A A B. The first two repetitions are the same and the third starts the same but ends differently. In a solo, you can use this on a smaller scale. For example:

3

Track 3.1

SEQUENCE

Repeat the motif on a different scale degree. Remember the "golden rule of repetition!"

4

Track 3.2

INVERT

Turn it upside down.

5

Track 3.3

RETROGRADE

Play it backwards. Jimmy Hendrix perfected this to the degree that it sounded like a tape being played backwards. Okay—so it's a little esoteric. But it works!

6

Track 3.4

SHIFTED RHYTHM

Start the motif in a different place in the bar.

7

Track 3.5

NOTE:

An exception to the *"golden rule of repetition"* is that, after five or six repetitions, the interest curve rises. This is common practice in the blues and makes a great climax.

FRAGMENT

Cut and paste. Use little pieces of the motif to make a larger shape. Stretch it, compress it, make it "stutter."

8

Track 3.6

NON-MOTIVIC MATERIAL AND ITS USES

Not everything you play will be a motif. Between statements of motifs, the first option is to rest. Just let the rhythm section, or your left hand, maintain the pulse, feel and texture. This is called using *space*. A second option is to play a groove figure—anything from short quarter notes in the style of Freddy Green to a funk-motor figure or Latin *guajeo* (dance rhythm)—in other words, join the rhythm section momentarily.

A third option is to use some kind of "connective tissue:" sweep, a glissando, scale or pattern of any length leading into the beginning of the motif.

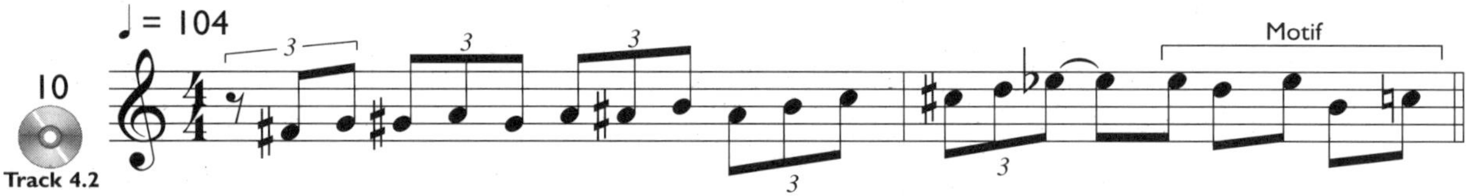

Or, try a "trail-off" growing out of the end of the motif.

Also, for a more sophisticated, higher intensity (and more jazz oriented) format, motivic material can be connected by scales, patterns and freely invented material.

Some Thoughts

Make the motion of your line balanced and logical. Don't end on the tonic ("1" of the scale) until the end of the solo, if you must at all. Ending phrases with a leap or scale segment (final note staccato as in example 11) leaves the listener anticipating the next phrase.

THE DOUBLE MELODIC LINE AND ITS USES

For added interest and a bigger, more complex sound, try thinking of your right hand as playing a double melodic line (two melodies at once).

> The recommended tempo for all the examples on this page is ♩ = 112.

REITERATED PEDAL TONE

A *pedal tone* is a sustained or continuously repeated tone.

13
Track 5.1

Example 13 combines this pedal tone: ...and this melody:

14
Track 5.2

RUDIMENTAL DRUMMING STRUCTURES

Here's one based on a *paradiddle* (a drum rudiment where strokes alternated as follows: RLRR LRLL).

R = Right
L = Left

15
Track 5.3

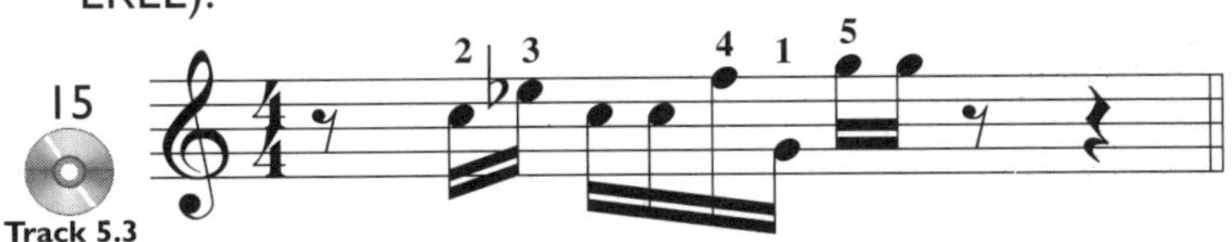

Example 15 combines this: and this:

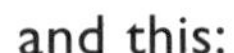

16
Track 5.4

CALL AND RESPONSE

Call and response with the hand jumping from one register to another gives the effect of more than one player. Example 17 has a riff alternating with improvisation.

17
Track 5.5

SOME USEFUL PATTERNS

The following patterns are useful for building motifs and connective tissue. Experiment and find personal ways of doing each of these in the chromatic, diatonic and blues scales, ascending and descending and in all keys. Also, you should invent many patterns of your own.

The recommended tempo for all the examples on this page is ♩ = 144.

Diads sequenced up the scales.

Triads

Four-Note Sequence

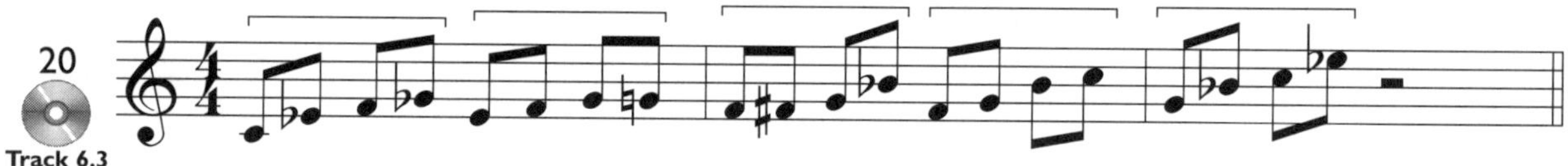

Broken 3rds

Broken 4ths

A Word About Patterns:

Don't let them become mechanical. Vary them by superimposing unusual rhythms, inserting rests, repeated notes and repeating fragments.

PERMUTATIONS

Any group of notes can be put through *permutations* (re-orderings) and then applied to a scale. In the first measure of example 23, for instance, a three-note motif including C (1), E♭ (♭3) and F (4) of the C Minor Pentatonic scale is put through six permutations in a measure of $\frac{6}{4}$ time. The measure starts on C (1). In the second measure, all six permutations are repeated, this time starting on the next note in the C Minor Pentatonic scale, E♭ (♭3). If we think of the six permutations as one line, then the second measure is a sequence of the first. We can think of the second measure as being in the 2nd Mode of the minor pentatonic scale (you can think of any scale as having modes). Whew! Then, there is a third repetition on the 3rd Mode. This is an excellent exercise for developing facility with any scale or set of chord tones.

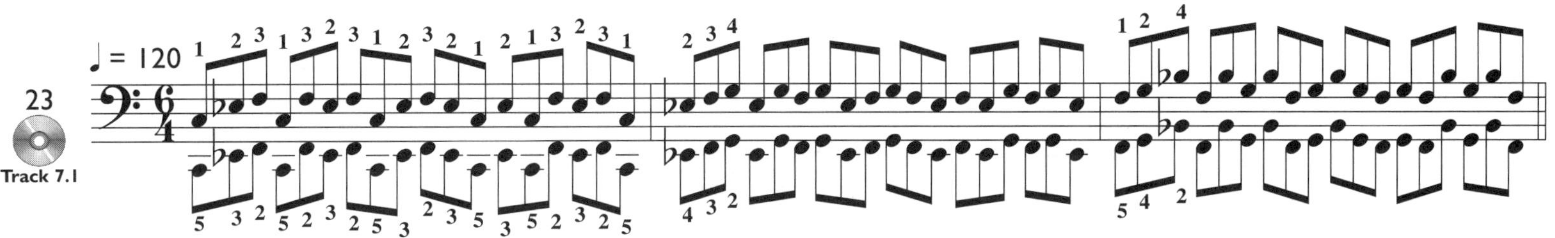

In the next example, put these fingerings, or modes of the C Pentatonic scale, through the same permutations as in example 23.

The figure in example 25 is good for another effect: the *flurry*. A flurry is a group of fast notes that makes the audience think, "Wow, this person can play!" The three-note permutations from example 23 are put through the blues scale, but the root rises chromatically on each group of three! If this makes your brain hurt, it's okay. Just spend some time gazing at examples 23 and 25 and it'll click eventually.

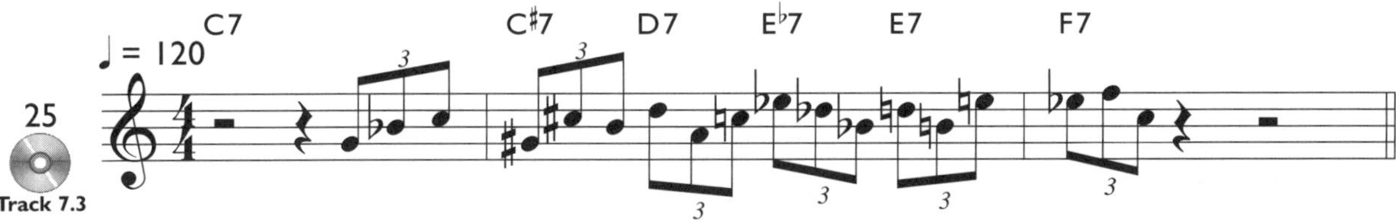

Here's another example of a flurry using two, two-note units (F and G♭; F and E):

REAL IMPROVISATION—INVENTING MATERIAL AS YOU SOLO

Hopefully, the ideas below will fire your imagination. They also show how really cool stuff can come from a simple idea. Think of these as "devices" which you should have in your "bag."

Repeated tone followed by scale (or arpeggio):

Repeated tone as an arrival point of arpeggio (or scale):

Leap followed by scale in opposite direction:

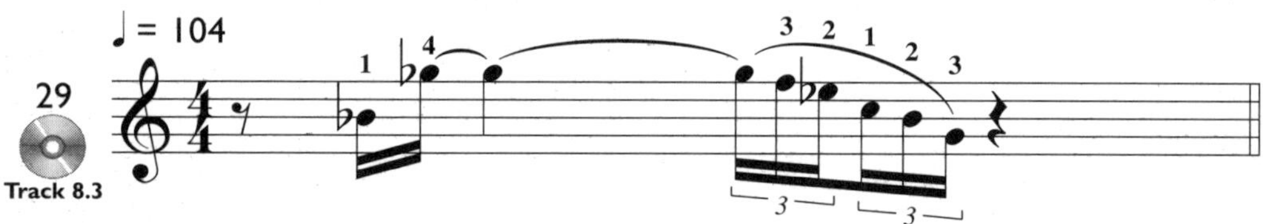

Embellishments on successive chord or scale tones:

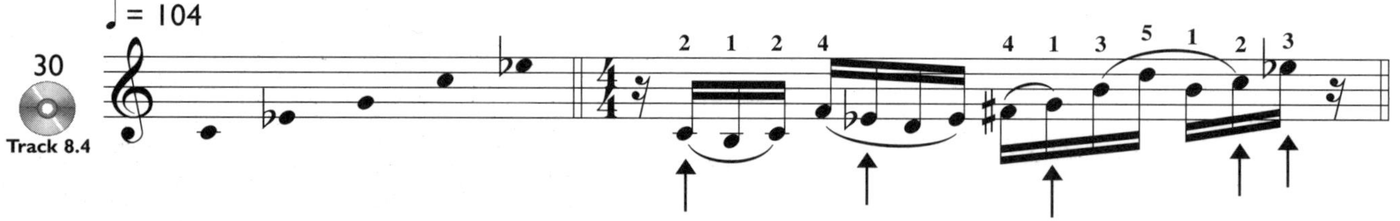

Two alternating tones followed by a leap:

Fingers Aflame, on page 25, has two choruses using some of these ideas.

> *Exercise:*
> Take two or three of these ideas and try to play a continuous line alternating them for as long as possible.

Track 9

FINGERS AFLAME

CHANGING HARMONIC DENSITY

Listeners hear a melody as a band of sound. It can be a thin band of sound (single note line) or a thicker band of sound. It can be made thicker by harmonizing, or duplicating, the line with a specific interval in parallel motion. In Chapter 2, page 20 of *Intermediate Blues Keyboard*, you learned a classic blues lick with notes harmonized in 3rds mid-way through.

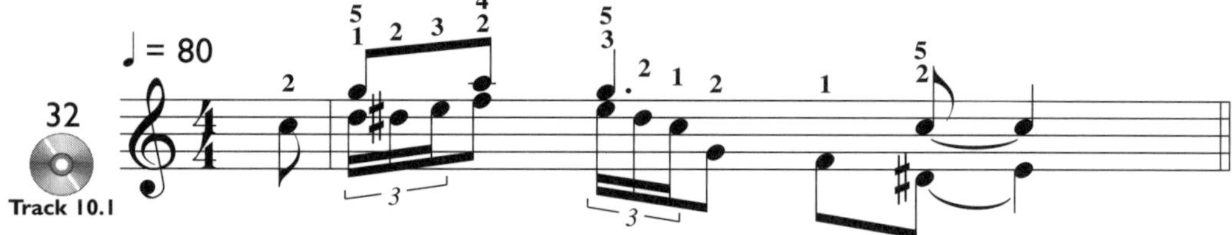

This kind of harmonization of a line, or portions of a line, creates interest by varying the color of the line, underscoring important motivic ideas, distinguishing separate voices in hockets or "call and response" structures, or just by adding bright highlights in unexpected places.

Try using longer passages in 3rds.

Example 34 uses 4ths.

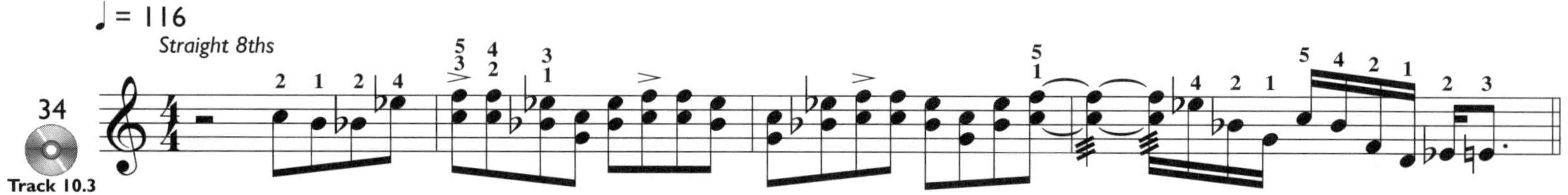

Harmonizing in 6ths makes a very sweet sound.

Octaves are effective, too.

To make the harmonic density of your moving lines even wider, duplicate them in 3rds, 6ths and 4ths at the same time. That brings us to our next topic, *block voicing*.

BLOCK VOICING

To get the maximum intricacy and variety of color and texture in your playing, imitate the big band sound. The main stylistic device you should adopt is saxophone-section-type block voicing. Here some ways you can do this:

Single Hand—Triadic

The recommended tempo for all the examples on this page is ♩ = 104.

Single Hand—Added Note or 7th Chord Voicings

Two Hands Locked (George Shearing's innovation)

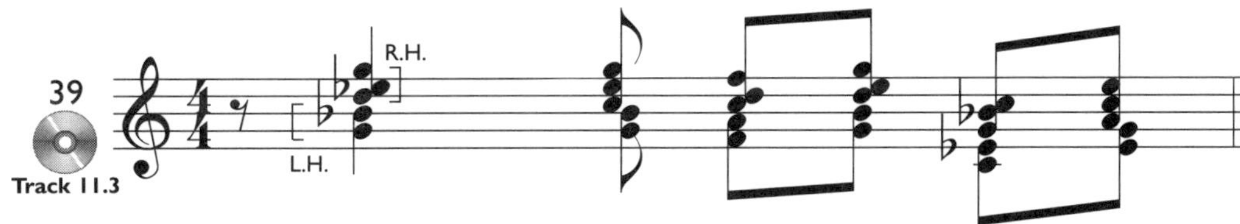

Two Hands Harmonized at the Octave

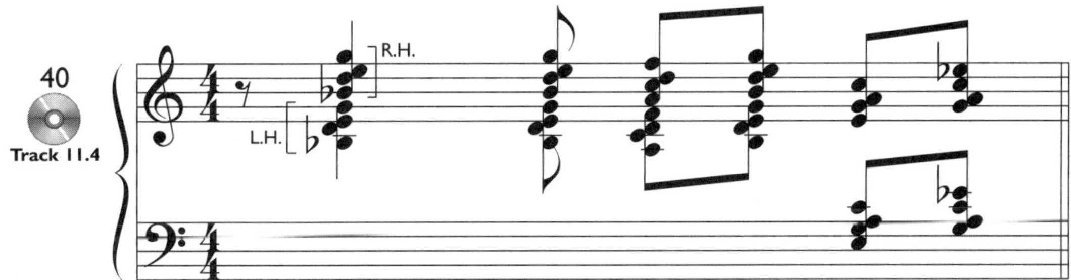

"Poor Man's Block Voicing"—Right-Hand Melody in Octaves with the Left-Hand Chord Voicing Played in Rhythmic Unison

Here is a composition imitating a big band and demonstrating some of these types of block voicing. The chords in the last two measures require the reach of a 10th. If this is impractical for you, roll the chords.

THE INCREDIBLE EXPANDING RIFF

Track 12

C9
F9
C9
R.H.
L.H.
GAug7,♯9
C7,♯9,13
F13
R.H.
L.H.
A♭Maj7/B♭
Play D♯ with side of the thumb.
C7
R.H.
L.H.
R.H.
E♭7/A
Dmin11
L.H.
GAug7,♯9
C9
ff
Gmin11
G♭13
F9
EAug5,9
E♭13
D7,♭9
D♭9
C9

CHAPTER 3

Variety in Turnarounds and Progressions

TRITONE SUBSTITUTION

Substituting one chord for another is one of the most important tools we have for varying a blues progression. One of the most popular substitutions is the *tritone substitution*. Any dominant 7th chord can be replaced with another dominant 7th chord whose root is three whole steps—a tritone—away. This works because the 3rd and the 7th of any dominant 7th chord are also the 7th and 3rd, repectively, of the dominant 7th chord a tritone away. For instance, the 3rd of a C7 chord is E. The 7th of the G♭7 chord is F♭, the enharmonic equivalent of E. The 7th of the C7 is B♭, which is also the 3rd of the G♭7.

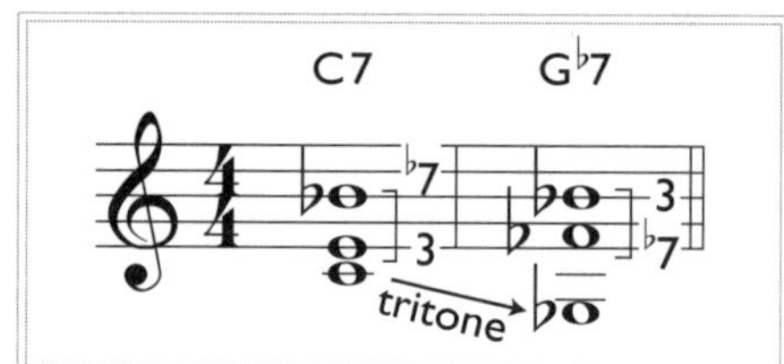

So, to make your blues progression more interesting, the dominant 7th chord on V can be replaced by a dominant 7th chord on the ♭2 (you learned an ending like this in *Intermediate Blues Keyboard*). And, in any cycle of 5ths progression of dominant chords, such as vi-ii-I, any chord can be replaced by its tritone substitute.

We can apply this to the I-vi-ii-V turnaround. Below is a chart showing the possibilities.

TABLE OF TRITONE SUBSTITUTIONS FOR I-vi-ii-V IN C

I	vi	ii	V
C	A7	D7	G7
C	A7	A♭7	G7
C	A7	A♭7	D♭7
C	A7	D7	D♭7
C	E♭7	D7	G7
C	E♭7	D7	D♭7
C	E♭7	A♭7	G7
C	E♭7	A♭7	D♭7

Most of these should sound familiar to you since they are frequently used. Many other variations are possible.

Exercise:

Try: 1) using two changes per measure by including substitutions;
2) starting the cycle of 5ths in a different place than vi;
3) putting a iimin7 chord before any V7 chord;
4) inserting root movement of a 3rd or 2nd anywhere in a cycle of 5ths progression.

These procedures should help you invent new chord progressions for some time to come.

The table below shows common substitutions used in a twelve-bar blues. These are by no means all the possibilities, but they'll get you started on your own path to discovering others. The chart is divided into twelve equal sections, each one representing a bar of the twelve-bar blues. There are four beats per bar. Except where noted, two chords in a bar means there are two beats per chord, four chords means one beat per chord.

SUBSTITUTIONS FOR THE TWELVE-BAR BLUES

C7-I							
C7	G♭7	F7		C7		Gmin7	C7
		F7	F♯dim7			C7	G♭7
C		Bmin7♭5	E7	Amin7	D7	Gmin7	G♭7
		E7		F7	F♯dim	Gmin7	C7
		E7		A7		D7 G7	Gmin7 C7
C7	F7	B♭7	E♭7	A♭7	D♭7	F♯7	B7
F7-IV				**C7-I**			
		F♯dim				A7	
		B♭7				E♭7	
		B♭7	Bdim			E♭m7	A♭m7
						Am7♭5	D7
				C7	B7	B♭7	A7
F7	B♭7	E♭7	D7 D♭7	C7	F7	B♭7	E♭7
				C7	B7	E7	E♭7
				C7	F7	B♭7	E♭7
G7-V		**F7-IV**		**C7-I**		**G7-V**	
Dmin7		G7					
Dmin7	G7						
		Cmin7	F7	B♭min7	E♭7	A♭min7	D♭7
		A♭7	G7		A7	D7	G7
		Dmin7♭5	G7		B♭7	A♭7 G7	
					C7/E	F	F♯dim
				C7/E		F	B♭7
A7	D7	A♭7	D♭7	C G7*		G7	

*This chord falls on the second beat of the bar.

Two closing thoughts:

1) Notice how the blues scale notes (G, B♭, C, E♭) become more colorful over the G♭7 chord, which is the tritone substitution for the tonic chord. They become ♭9 (G or A𝄫), 3 (B♭), ♯11 (C) and 13 (E♭).

2) On an historical note, Art Tatum invented new chord progressions as he was improvising —something to work towards.

CHAPTER 4

Multiple Functions of the Hands and Independence

In Chapter 2 we dealt briefly with the double melodic line as a way of increasing interest and complexity. In this chapter, we'll look at some devices for more sophisticated comping. First, let's expand on a classic blues lick you learned in *Intermediate Blues Keyboard*, where the tonic is sustained against a simple motif.

In this book, everything should be played with a swing feel unless marked "*Straight 8ths*."

Sustaining the 6th can also work in this structure.

Try it with the 3rd.

It can also work with one of any two adjacent 3rds in any chord. For example, here's the concept applied in four ways through a C9 chord:

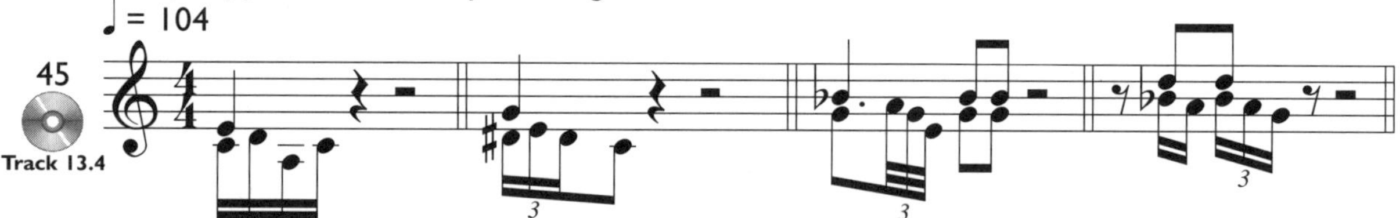

From supporting a motif with a single note, we move to sustaining one note and, with the same hand, using the other notes in the chord to play time or comp.

Similarly, we can play a melody or repeated single note with the thumb while the other fingers comp or play a bass line.

A more complex strategy would be "tiling the plane" with interlocking rudimental patterns. For instance, take this pattern:

Combine it with this one, which is really just the inversion of the first:

You get something like this:

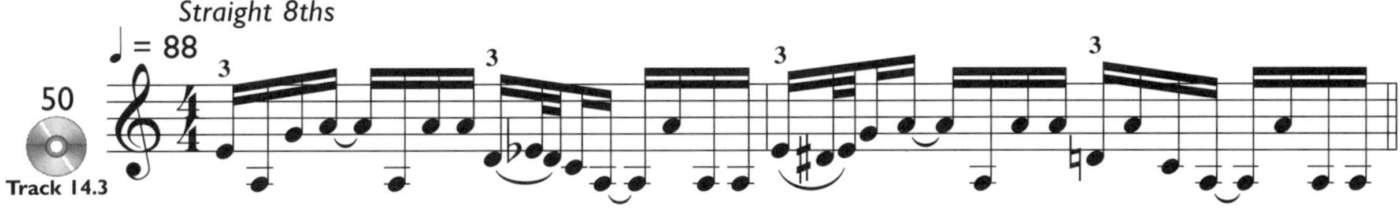

There is also an important multiple function for the left hand. We can alternate between a bass line and chordal accompaniment.

Here is an example in the style of New Orleans blues:

Here's an example of the same technique, but this time in a Rhythm and Blues (R&B) context:

INDEPENDENCE

Independence is the ability to simultaneously play completely different things in each hand. In group situations, if you have good independence you can add another layer of texture to the overall sound. This is also a very useful thing when you are playing solo. Here are a series of exercises that, if used as prescribed, will allow you to learn to improvise freely over any bass line or ostinato (an accompaniment figure that is repeated).

Step 1. Practice the bass line with your metronome until it is completely comfortable and doesn't require all of your attention.

Step 2. As you play the bass line in the left hand, play an eighth-note chord tone in the right hand (root or 5th are good choices) on the downbeat. Do this eight times. Then, strike the right-hand note on the "&" of "1" eight times. Then move on to the "2," etc. Do this on every eighth-note pulse in the bar. Be sure your metronome is still on, set to a slow tempo.

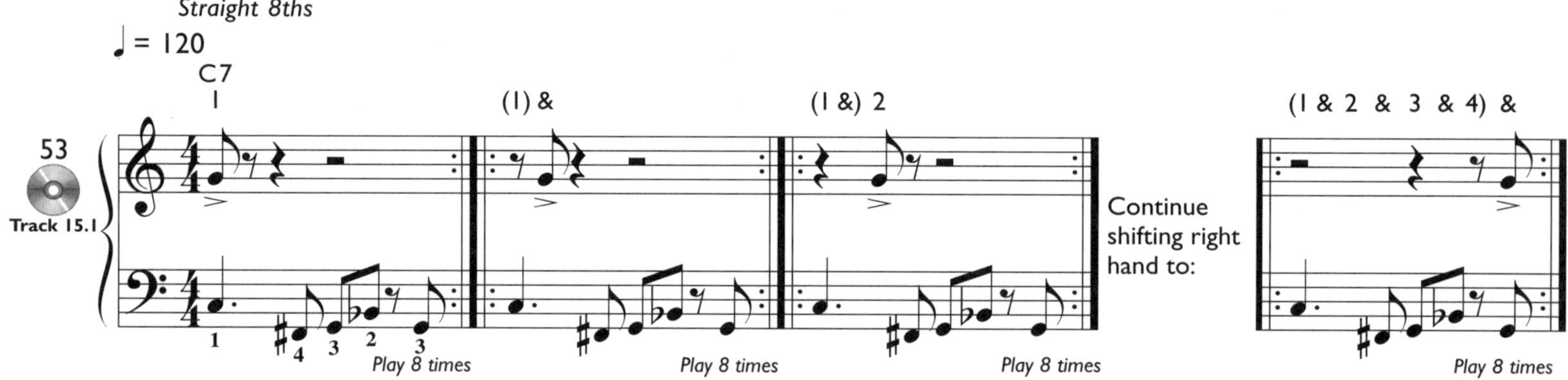

Step 3. Now, hit on every eighth with the right hand while repeating the bass line in the left. Do this until it is comfortable.

Step 4. Now alternate your right-hand pitch with its upper neighboring tone in the scale until it flows. For now, let's assume we're using the G Dorian scale, because it works well over the bass.

Step 5. Then proceed to the next scale degree and alternate that with your starting pitch. Repeat this step with all the degrees of the scale between your starting pitch and the next octave.

Step 6. Repeat Steps 4 and 5, this time starting with a lower neighbor tone descending through the scale from there.

Step 7. Now repeat a three-note scale segment in the right hand while playing the bass line in the left. When you are comfortable with this, play the entire scale up to the interval of a 9th and back again, using a 1-2-3 thumb-under fingering. Repeat until secure.

Step 8. Now attempt simple right-hand patterns (refer to page 22 and your own notebook) over the bass line, still using eighth notes. Start with simple patterns (broken 3rds, broken 4ths, etc.) and work towards more complex and more *syncopated* patterns. Practice syncopation on every beat in the bar or bars.

PHOTO • COURTESY OF THE INSTITUTE OF JAZZ STUDIES

***James Edward "Jimmy" Yancey** is thought by many to be the master of boogie-woogie, but his quiet stage demeanor did not lend itself to stardom, and he did not tour or record as prolifically as his own protogées. On the bandstand, Jimmy frequently provided accompaniment to his wife, a vocalist, Estelle "Mama" Yancey. Despite Jimmy Yancey's subdued nature, his music was part of the boogie-woogie craze of the 1930s. Jimmy Yancey is respected by both blues and jazz enthusiasts as a master of his art.*

IMPROVISING YOUR WALKING BASS LINES

Like any proficient bass player, when playing left hand (or organ pedal) walking bass lines, you should be able to play an interesting new line every chorus. Here are some helpful things to bear in mind:

WALKING BASS CONSIDERATIONS

1. The easiest way to make a walking bass line is to use these scale degrees:
   Ascending—1-2-♯2-3
   Descending—8-7-6-5.

   Both allow an easy route away from or towards the tonic.

2. If your chord progression root is moving up a 4th, it is only necessary to make sure the 7th degree in your line agrees with the 7th of the first chord.

3. The first chord can be either major or minor, since ♯2 is the same as ♭3 and 3 can be a chromatic passing tone leading to the root of the next chord.

4. On a minor chord where the root movement is not a 4th, you can use 1-♯1-2-♭3.

59

Track 17.1

SOME OTHER POSSIBILITIES

CHORDAL OUTLINE

When outlining triads, repeat one note to get a four-beat bar. With 7th chords, avoid the 7th at the end of the bar unless:

1. it's a leading tone to the next root; or
2. the next chord is being played in 1st inversion (with the 3rd in the bass).

60

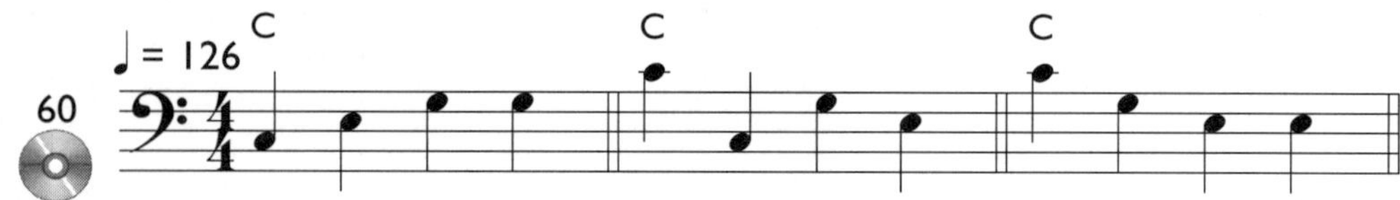

Track 17.2

ANY COMBINATION OF OCTAVES AND 5THS

Also octaves and 5ths with lower chromatic neighboring tones.

CHORDAL OUTLINE WITH PASSING TONES

You can use actual passing tones to connect the chord tones (all stepwise motion) or skip up or down to non-chord tones (as long as they resolve to chord tones).

FLAMS

Keep your bass line alive and interesting by inserting occasional eighth notes, triplet eighths, and, most importantly, *flams*. The flam (grace note) can be almost anything. Some possibilities include:

The previous bass note
The same pitch as the bass note
Any chordal tone, an out of the key escape tone
A right-hand chord or
Part of a chord in either hand
Anything else you can think of!

Below are some examples of *flams*. Notice that they can be written either as grace notes or as actual rhythms. They can even include multiple notes. Let these examples spur your imagination, then come up with some of your own. Have fun!

Exercise:
Apply each walking bass device on pages 36 and 37 to all the tunes with walking bass lines in the last few chapters. Try them with pairs of chords, particularly ii7 – V7, and cycle of 5ths progressions. Cozy-up to this area of study—spend some time with it every day.

TIP:
To sound more "bass-like," play written bass lines down an octave whenever possible.

COMBINING IDEAS

In Chapter 4 of *Intermediate Blues Keyboard*, you were introduced to the idea of creating bass lines by mixing walking lines with other devices, such as shuffle patterns. Here's an example of this kind of line:

64 Track 19

Your solo playing will be much more interesting if, on some tunes, you expand on this idea and alternate lines that are even more diverse. Masters of this technique include Earl Hines, Meade Lux Lewis, Errol Garner and Art Tatum. In a single chorus, you might alternate a few bars of a groove figure with:

A bar or two of stop time (left hand silent or sustaining the chord – right hand in flight)
A melodic statement (or response) in octaves
A *hammered* (struck repeatedly) interval root and 5th broken up by chords
A broken octave pedal point
A swirling chromatic scale connecting one root to the next
A vigorous trill
Marcato (accented) left-hand chords
Etc.!

PHOTO • COURTESY OF THE INSTITUTE OF JAZZ STUDIES

*The legendary and innovative **Earl "Fatha Hines**, born in 1903, spent the better part of the 20th century at the top of the jazz piano heap.*

The possibilities are endless. Select or invent your own vocabulary of accompaniments, then set up your own exercises to develop this facility. Below is a very free application of this concept.

CRAZY QUILT

Track 20

TIP:
Each bass idea that you invent should be run through the exercises on pages 34 and 35, although a certain number could be done under a trill, tremolo or ostinato in the right hand.

Here is a composition using a New Orleans-style, multi-function left-hand part which gives the effect of repeated chords and a bass line in the left hand. *Your Indigo Purgatory* is in the style of the changes to *My Blue Heaven*. If you need to, roll the 10ths.

YOUR INDIGO PURGATORY

Track 21

Fmin
B♭/C
Fmin
A♭/B♭
Fmin
B♭/C
Fmin
A♭/B♭
E♭add2
E♭/G
A♭/B♭
E♭
A♭/B♭
D.S. al Coda
Coda
E♭
A♭/B♭
E♭
8va

Here is another New Orleans-style, multi-function left-hand figure in the style of James Booker. The effect here is a free bass line and repeated chords set in a more syncopated rhythm.

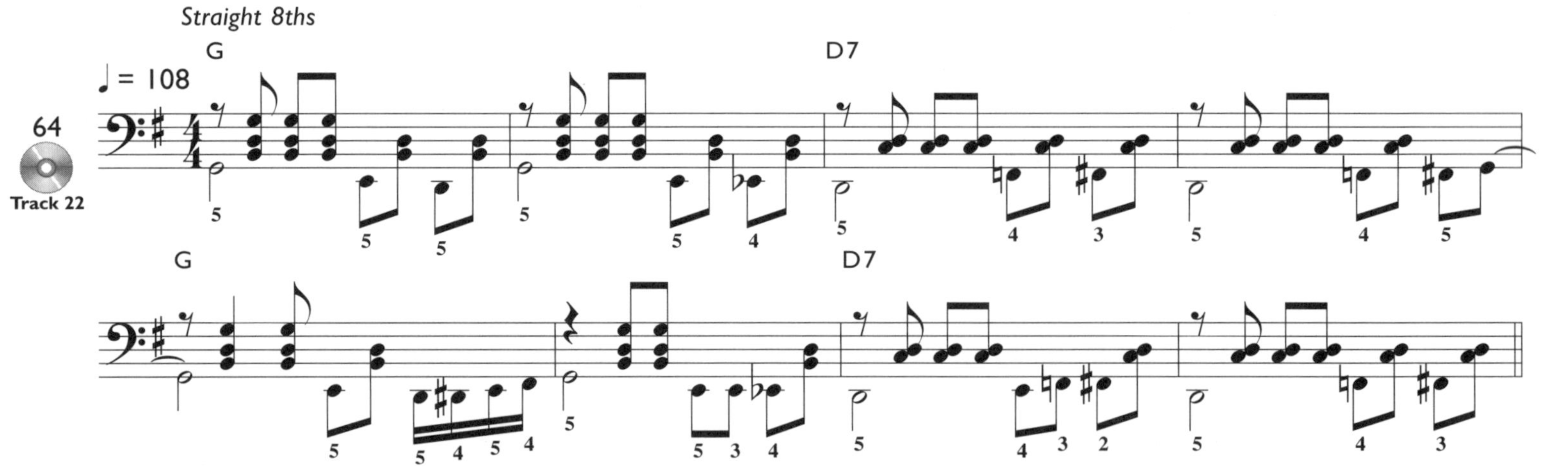

PHOTO • CHUCK PULIN/COURTESY OF STAR FILE,INC.

Mac Rebennack *soaked up the music of great New Orleans players like Professor Longhair, Fats Domino, Huey 'Piano' Smith and Allan Toussaint, and draped himself in the voodoo legends and symbolism of his city to become* ***Dr. John the Night Tripper****. His show introduced the psychedelic movement to New Orleans sounds and established him as a hip R&B artist with a Delta twist. He played guitar as a teenager but got shot in the hand, losing the use of his left index finger. Then James Booker helped him with his organ playing and he played his first keyboard gigs. Dr. John went on to work as a solo pianist, composer, singer, psychedelic rock star and producer.*

MORE ABOUT STRIDE

The recommended tempo for all the examples on this page is ♩ = 100.

In *Intermediate Blues Keyboard*, you learned the basics of stride: the left hand alternates between bass notes on beats 1 and 3 and a chord voicing on the backbeat (beats 2 and 4 of the bar). This was the style as developed by James P. Johnson. Fats Waller, who roomed with Johnson briefly when he was young, added a major innovation. Critics called what Waller was doing a "fist full of keys" approach to the piano. Instead of single bass notes on beats 1 and 3, he would play a 5th, 10th or big open position chord.

Instead of using single-note walking lines to connect stride patterns, Waller would play 10ths or even open position 7th chords.

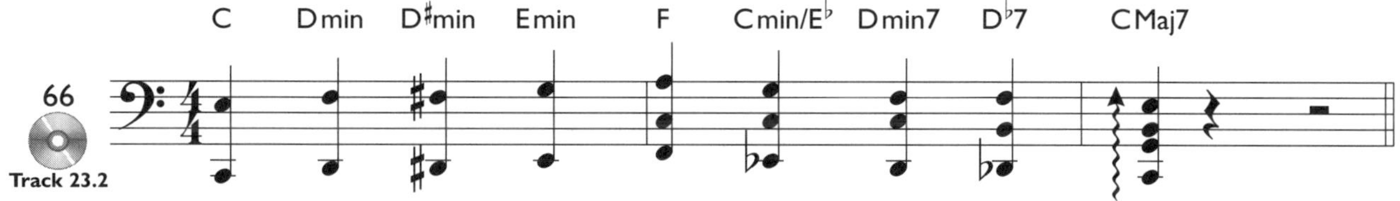

The sound of stride played well is massive, virtuosic and very entertaining. It is also a specialty that takes many long hours of practice to really master. If you are inclined, do the exercises below around the cycle of 5ths. Start very slowly. It is essential that you learn them by feel. Do them until you can play them with your eyes closed or your hands covered with a light cloth.

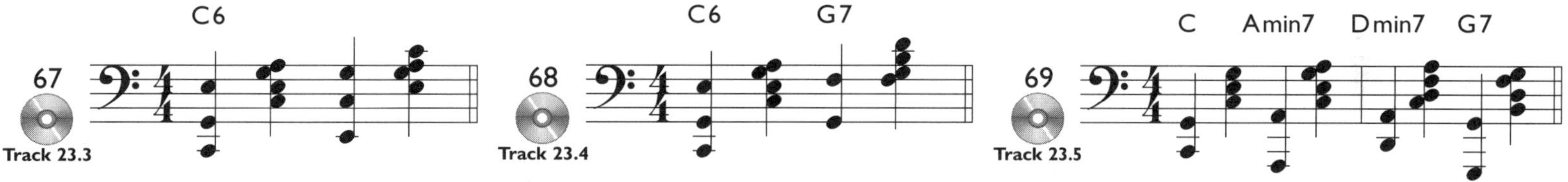

In the event that your time for practicing such things is limited, here are some thoughts about imitating the stride sound. First, use broken, open or closed position left-hand voicings. You will sacrifice mass and power, but you can maintain the motion and idea of stride. Second, using the multi-function ideas from pages 32 and 33, you can put the off beats in the lower part of the right hand, the upper part of the left hand, or both together. Also, in a difficult situation, simply playing a chord voicing on the appropriate melody note in the right hand can preserve the stride motion.

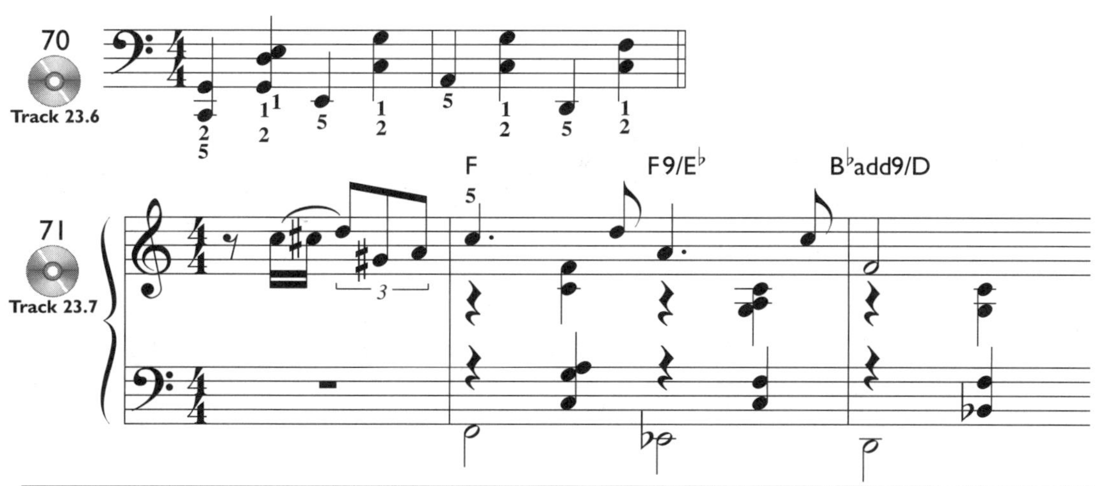

Here is a piece using stride (some real, some not so real) and some alternation of bass figures in the style of Art Tatum. Note the rhythm in measure 7. It's a quarter-note triplet subdivided into 16ths. Think of three quarters in the time of two, then subdivide.

GOD WAS IN THE HOUSE

Track 24

A

G Dmin6/F E7 A7 D6add9 Emin A♭7/E♭ D♭Maj7 C7 F♯min7♭5 B7

B♭7 Amin7 D7 G G♯min7 C♯Aug F♯ Bmin7 E7

B♭min7 E♭7 Amin7 D7 G B7 EAug7

B

A13 D7 Emin E♭7 Dmin D♭7 C7 B7

Bdim B♭min7 E♭7 Amin7 D7
To Coda
G
R.H.
L.H.
G Dmin7 G7 CMaj7 Bdim CAug/B♭ Amin A♭dim Gmin7 F♯7♭5
L.H.
L.H.
F13 Amin7 F7/C B♭min7 E♭ A♭min7 D♭ Gmin7 C7 F7 E7 B♭7
E♭7,♯11 D7 Cmin7/F F Bmin7 E7 B♭min7 E♭ Amin7 D7
8va
loco
D.S. al Coda
Coda
G6 G/B C7 C♯dim D F♯ G

CHAPTER 5

Blues Organ

The mighty Hammond B-3.

PHOTO • COURTESY OF STEVEN EAKOR, HAMMOND SUZUKI USA,INC.

When we talk about the organ in blues, R&B, gospel and jazz, we are referring primarily to the Hammond B-3. There is nothing really comparable to the B-3 sound. Although often imitated, nothing duplicates the sound of the B-3 with a Leslie speaker, and the history and development of Blues organ parallels the integration of the Hammond B-3 into popular music.

B-3 owners are an exclusive club. Besides an initial outlay of up to $8,000 for a mint condition organ with Leslie speaker, the organs are expensive to maintain, and, at more than 400 pounds for the organ plus 150 pounds for the Leslie, they are difficult to move. Since production of the original B-3 was discontinued in 1974, parts and service can be difficult to obtain. However, many players and listeners consider these challenges a small price to pay. In spite of advances in digital sampling keyboards, even a large sample library can't begin to equal the rainbow of sounds that a great B-3 player like Booker T. Jones can create as he plays.

From the beginning, organs have been intended to put all the sounds of the orchestra or band at the fingertips of a single player. The B-3 was originally intended as an alternative to pipe organs in churches and for use as an instrument in the home. The Leslie speaker, with its rotating horn and drum, was designed to imitate the sound of the pipe organ with pitches emanating from different pipes around the hall. The closest thing to a jazz big band is a "Texas organ trio"—a guitarist or saxophonist and a drummer fleshing out a keyboard player's pedal or left-hand bass, comping and soloing.

Rotating "tone wheels," each of which has from two to one-hundred-ninety-two notched teeth, generates the sound of a Hammond organ. As they turn, the notches create a fluctuation in a coil wound around a permanent magnet. A wheel with a higher number of notches produces a higher pitch. When the keys make contact, there is an audible click. While this sound was not popular in churches and homes, it gave an articulated attack that was much prized by players of rhythmic, driving music.

Some of the early Hammond organ players were Fats Waller, Count Basie and Wild Bill Davis. Some other noted players are Shirley Scott, Jack McDuff, Jackie Davis, Billy Preston, Dr. Lonnie Smith, Rosemary Bailey, John Patton, Milt Buchner, Joe Bucci, Jimmy McGriff, John Medeski (of Medeski, Martin & Wood), Joey DeFrancesco and, of course, the great Jimmy Smith. Collecting and studying recordings of this abbreviated list will give you a good start on developing a concept of what organ should sound like in a blues and jazz context.

Owners and prospective owners of Hammond organs are referred to the excellent book by Mark Vail, *The Hammond Organ – Beauty and the B,* published by Miller Freeman, United News and Media Publications, which treats history, workings and operating information in exhaustive detail.

A QUICK GUIDE TO OPERATING THE B-3

Here is the procedure for turning the organ on:

1. Put the *start switch* to the "on" position.

2. When the sound changes, release the start switch and turn on the *run switch*.

3. Give it time to warm up. Oil from two small reservoirs is actually working its way through the organ's moving parts.

The bottom octave of each of the two *manuals* (a manual is a keyboard—the B-3 has two) has the colors of the keys reversed. These are not notes. They are *presets*. A preset is a combination of settings used to get a particular sound. These can be achieved with one touch of a preset key.

Above the upper manual are two sets of *drawbars* arranged in four groups of nine each. Each drawbar mixes in a specific *overtone* from the lowest (corresponding to a sixteen-foot organ pipe) to the highest (corresponding to a one-foot organ pipe). An overtone is a *harmonic*—a lesser, higher tone that accompanies each *fundamental* tone. Each group of nine drawbars is color-coded in white, black and brown. When pushed all the way in, a drawbar does not affect the sound. If it is pulled out to "8," it produces its maximum effect. The specific combination of overtones is what creates familiar and new timbers. Manipulating these drawbars with one hand while you play with the other hand allows you to continuously vary your sound.

One of the features the Hammond is most famous for is the triggered percussion effect. This is a percussive sound that accompanies the attack of a note. It is found on the upper manual only. Four switches control this effect:

1. On/Off switch

2. Volume (normal and soft)

3. Decay time (fast or slow)

4. Two choices for the pitch of the harmonic above the note
    - the octave, which is called "second"
    - an octave and a 5th, which is called "third"

To trigger the percussion effect on every note, it is necessary to play staccato. Otherwise, only the first note of a phrase will have percussion added to it.

Post 1945 Hammonds have a four-position switch that gives three speeds of vibrato and an "Off" setting. Later models have a chorus effect added with three position labels: C1, C2 and C3.

GETTING STARTED WITH DRAWBAR SETTINGS

A good place to start for a bass sound is the 16' (sixteen foot, as in a sixteen foot organ pipe) drawbar on 8, $5^{1/3}$' on 2, 8' on 8. Experiment with coloring the sound by using some of the higher drawbars.

Most players start with the first three or four drawbars out and percussion on either setting. To increase the sound as you play additional choruses, try pulling out the highest drawbars more in each successive chorus. Or, move from high drawbars to low drawbars. By adding drawbars, you can swell the sound very similarly to what you can do with the volume pedal. When comping, avoid overpowering the soloist by not using the lowest drawbars. The Hammond Organ Company's manual advised against ever pulling all the drawbars all the way out. But the expression "pulling out all the stops" originated with organ players, and most players confess to having committed this sin at some time to compete with loud bands.

Individual drawbar settings are often jealously guarded secrets. *Hammond Organ – Beauty in the B* by Mark Vail lists the configurations of many famous organists.

IMPLICATIONS OF ORGAN KEYBOARD ACTION

Organ differs from piano in that the keys require less force to play. This means that *glissandos* (rapid scales played by sliding fingers over the keys) are much easier on organ. While piano glisses have to be done with the back of the 3rd finger fingernail or the thumb nail, organists can use almost any part of the finger or thumb and even the palms of their hands. These variations change the sound of the glissando and are a part of the B-3 vocabulary. Because of the ease with which they can be played, you can be very fanciful and imaginative in their use.

Some things organists can do are:

Multiple glisses hand over hand.

Glissandos in contrary motion (one hand going up and one hand going down simultaneously).

Climbing or falling zigzags with a single hand or changing hands with the changes of direction.

Grand sweeps to the beginning of a motif.

Fall-offs at the end of a phrase.

Sags (a gliss down from a note or chord of any size, and then up again returning to the same note or chord).

Short upward or downward glisses on every note of a scale or arpeggiated passage.

To make the note or chord at the end of an adventurous gliss more secure, have the other hand play the end note of the gliss, and put it in position as you gliss with the other hand.

A second benefit of easy keyboard action is speed. Jimmy Smith is probably one of the fastest musicians who ever lived. This is due to both his amazing technique and, in some part, to the instrument he chose to play. Organ keys return to position very quickly which allows for rapid reiteration of notes and chords. This makes trills very easy. More so than with piano, an organist can imitate the sounds of hand drums or even a trap set by using rudimental rhythm patterns between hands or fingers.

In this book, everything should be played with a swing feel unless marked "*Straight 8ths.*"

When soloing, think of your right hand as a horn player. The left hand is then free to vary the sound by changing drawbar settings, vibrato and chorus. Because organ pitches sustain indefinitely, you can use long notes that would just die away if you were playing piano. A long note at the peak of a line, with a scale leading into it and out of it, makes a good climax.

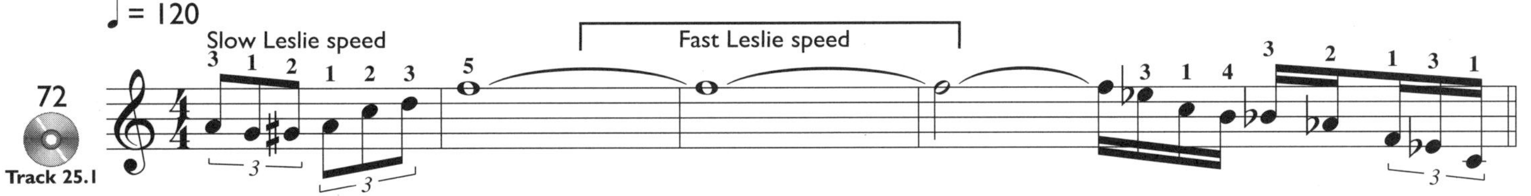

For a heavier climax, use an *inverted pedal point* (a high note held as the harmony changes underneath) and end with a descending scale or gliss.

Don't forget to let your lines breathe in a human manner so that listeners can digest what you play phrase by phrase. This will also give the listener a rest from the color of the instrument, however briefly, so they won't tire of the sound as quickly. Because there is no sustain pedal, as there is on the piano, it is good to occasionally hold a note or notes in the line as discussed in Chapter 4 with the multiple function of the hand exercises.

IMPLICATIONS OF KEYBOARD ACTION IN COMPING

The recommended tempo for all the examples on this page is ♩ = 72.

When creating backgrounds, the organ's sustain allows you to imitate the string orchestra. For harmonic continuity, keep your voicings in this register: F below middle C to G above middle C.

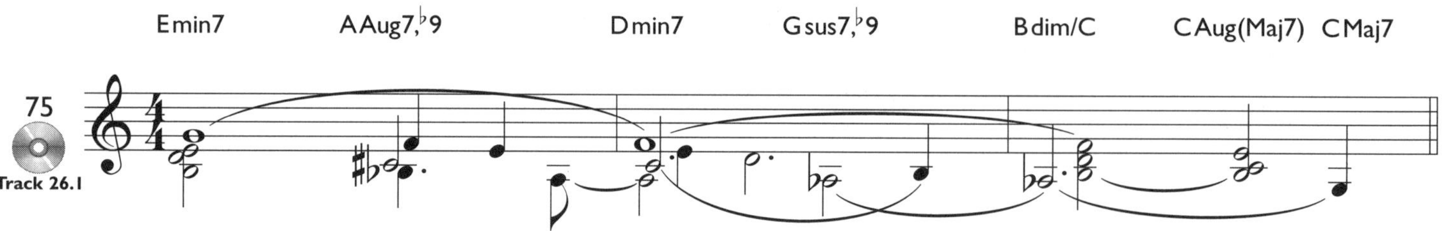

Think of each note as an individual voice or section of the string orchestra. Embellish a note before it moves.

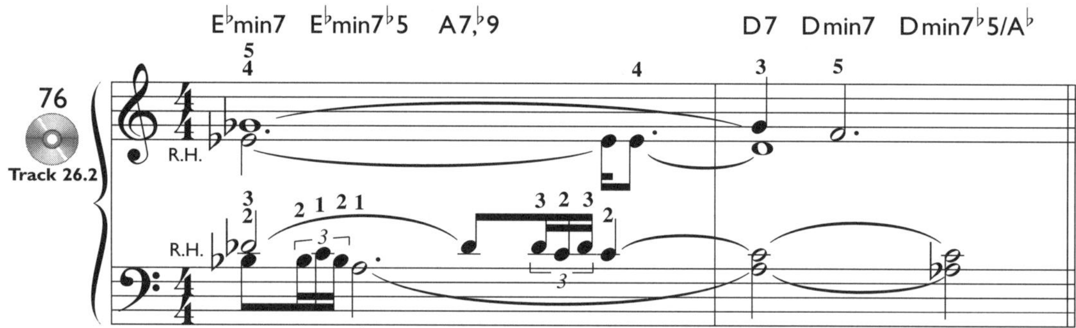

When a note moves more than a step, connect it to the following pitch with a chromatic or diatonic scale.

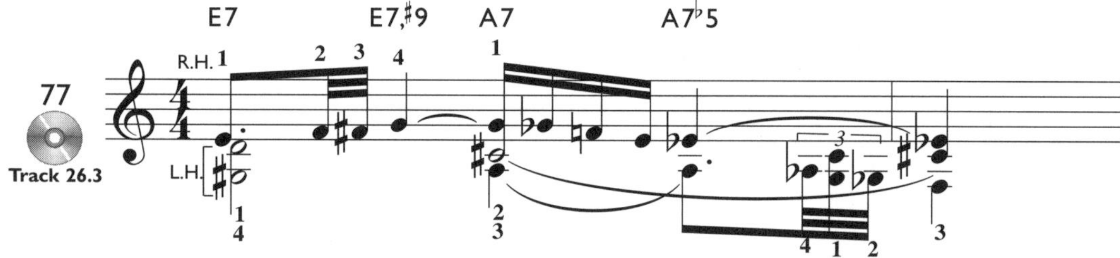

Sustain some notes of a chord and simultaneously tremolo others.

These devices will make listeners aware of single voices as they would be with real strings. Be sure to taper your chords with the swell pedal or drawbar registration to emulate one of the major characteristics of live strings. Splitting string sounds between the manuals will also give your strings sound more depth.

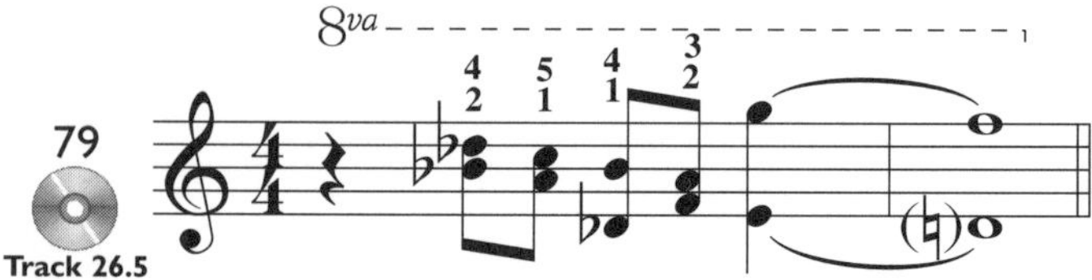

Descant-style (a high part above the melody) upper-register lines in single notes, or harmonized in parallel 3rds, 6ths or 10ths can be very effective. Keep the drawbar registration light and use chorus, vibrato and reverb to enhance the string-like effect.

For riffing and punch chords, think brass. Big sounds, heavy registration, edgy sounds, short note punctuations and interjections, two-handed tremolos in the style of the Basie Band's are the vocabulary to draw on here. This is a good time to review the block voicing material in Chapter 2.

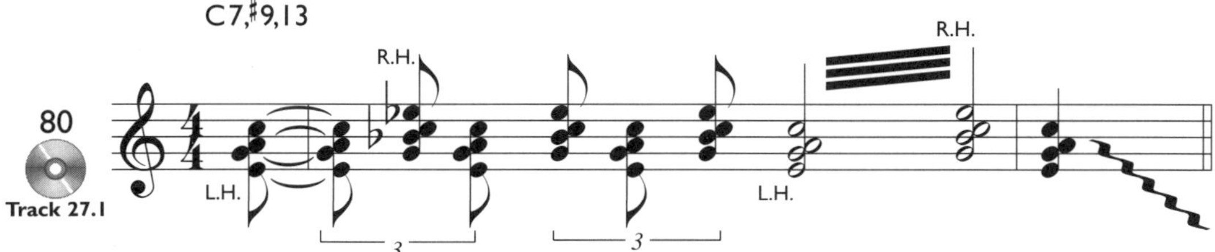

The recommended tempo for all the examples on this page is ♩ = 120.

A very effective device to use in conjunction with the percussion feature, is *clipping*. Hit a full chord or even a diatonic cluster (all the notes in a scale segment played simultaneously) and quickly release all but one or two notes.

The held notes can merely last longer than the rest of the chord or can be the beginning of the next line.

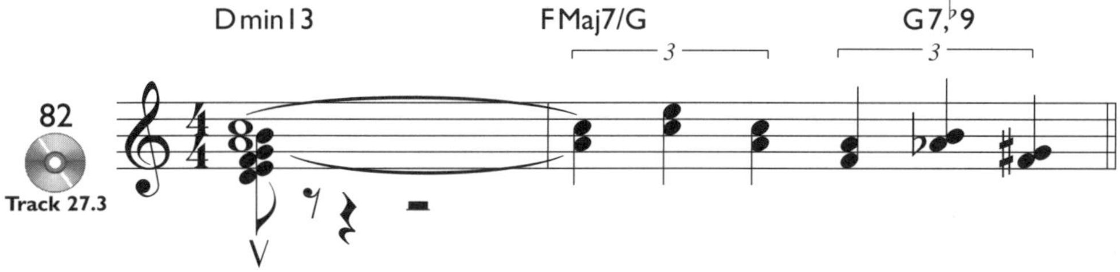

As with any serious musical study, you must acquaint yourself with the body of work that has accumulated for the instrument. Collect CD's, records and tapes from the masters mentioned in this chapter and listen, listen, listen, so you will begin the lifelong process of assimilating their achievements.

CHAPTER 6

Rhythm Section Playing, Comping and Grooving

PLAYING IN A BAND

The more people in the band, the less you play. Here are some other good rules of thumb:

- Just because you can play the bass line with the bass player doesn't mean you should.
- If both you and the guitarist comp at the same time, the end result will be rigid and very possibly rhythmically and harmonically cluttered (unless you are both extremely sensitive and ear training experts).
- Doubling any part of a drum figure may occasionally be desirable as a coloristic effect but, unless you give it your undivided attention, chances are good it will lack precision and obscure the pulse.
- An amplified keyboard (organ, synthesizer or piano), unless used judiciously, can cloud the air around any horn section.
- Most importantly, don't play all the time. This would make the band monochromatic. Listeners never have a chance to miss you if you're always in their faces!

It can be very effective to duplicate one or two notes of a bass line and occasionally double the bass in an ensemble passage when no one is soloing. Don't be heavy-handed about this. If the bass player glares at you, you should probably cease and desist. For the sake of clarity, it is best to mostly stay out of the bass player's register. This will also avoid tuning problems, particularily if the bassist is playing string bass or fretless bass guitar. Your left hand voicing in the comping register (F below middle C to G above middle C) and a fat bass note make a complete picture. Nothing else is necessary.

Two instruments comping simultaneously is usually wasted color. With few exceptions, the arranger's rule is "doubled notes are wasted notes." When working with another keyboard player or guitarist, trade off comping and filling functions or just take turns resting. A single comper allows for more rapid and effective responses to what the soloist is doing. If you stay alert, you and your fellow compers can develop the empathy to make fascinating and unpredictable changes in function and orchestration without stepping on each other's toes.

In a small group format, it is often appropriate to double the backbeat. In larger goups, it becomes more rare. It is more effective to add another unique rhythmic layer. A high keyboard pitch could, for instance, play a Latin rhythm (read about the *clavé rhythm* in Chapter 8). Or one could play a repeated figure in staccato, quarter-note triplets (in the mid-range and omitting the first beat) to add an unobtrusive layer. Always strive for a carefully balanced volume. Let taste and reserve be your guides.

If you double the horn section, your rhythmic precision (attacks and durations) as well as your volume level must be at the same level of perfection that horn players generally demand of themselves. Responses to horn riffs and punches are safer and more entertaining to hear. Other strategies are sweeps into, trail-offs from and flams before horn section figures. Again, don't overdo it.

Don't forget the comper's prime directive: ***make the soloist sound great and don't get in the way***. All the things you do to create a climax in your own solos can be used when comping. If you can insert the right device at the right moment at the right volume to put the soloist over the top, you will be in demand.

GROOVE

Feel, or groove, comes from maintaining a steady, predictable pulse and then tugging or pulling against that pulse. *Laying back* (playing slightly behind each beat) creates a relaxed feel, and playing on the front part of the beat creates an edgy and exuberant feel. The rhythm section creates one tonal/rhythmic plane and the soloist creates a second. The friction between these two generates groove. As the two move in tandem, sharing the same pulse, the soloist is free to break formation by playing one or more of the following:

Cross rhythms (rhythms with accents that do not coincide with those of the rhythm section)

83

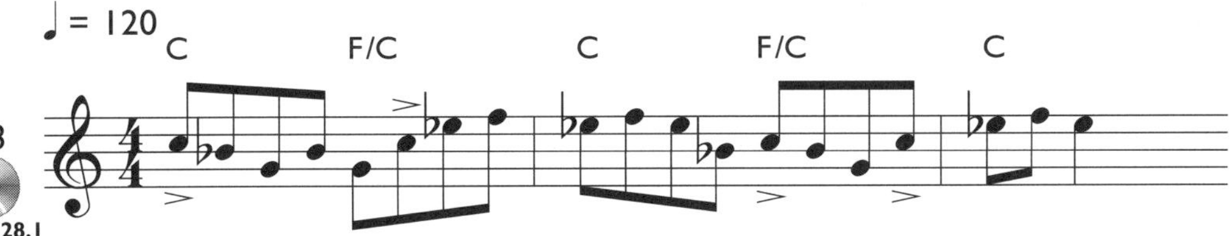

Track 28.1

> In this book, everything should be played with a swing feel unless marked "*Straight 8ths.*"

Hemiolas (making rhythmic groupings that have a different downbeat than the band's meter, such as groups of three in common time, or, as in this case, something more unusual, such as groups of seven notes in common time).

84

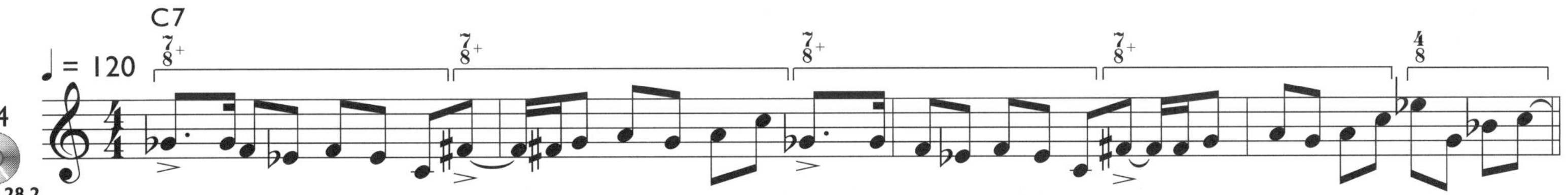

Track 28.2

Polyrhythms (two completely different tempos played simultaneously—the soloist plays a different rhythm/tempo than the rhythm section). Example 85 shows a 5 against 2 rhythm (5:2) in $\frac{3}{4}$ time.

85

Track 28.3

All of these devices allow the soloist to pull the listener away from the rhythm section's pulse and replace it momentarily with another. This creates tension which is released when the soloist returns to the rhythm section's pulse. The simplest illustration of this principle is the well-worn device of playing a series of off-beat quarter notes. Listeners attempting to track the beat are pulled to the off-beats with the soloist and, whether or not they can keep their toes tapping on the beat, they recognize the original pulse when the off-beats stop. This game is very entertaining.

86

Track 28.4

VOCAL ACCOMPANIMENT IN A DUO FORMAT

For many pianists, accompanying a good singer is one of their favorite activities. The challenge of supplying the bass line, changes, fills and a workable musical conception is the source of the thrill. In addition to all we have discussed about comping behind a soloist, ideally the complete accompanist should be flexible enough to play well in all keys. They should also know the singer's voice well enough to choose keys that exploit the tonal colors of its various registers. Positioning a critical note exactly on the singer's *break* between chest voice and head voice can move the performance from "ho-hum" to gut wrenching. Moving a low passage down a step, or even a half step, can sometimes put enough gravel in the voice to add an aura of sincerity to a confession of love or lust.

Playing behind a melody with words opens up the possibility of *tone painting*. The vocal literature of the blues is replete with moaning train whistles, visits to honky tonks and speakeasies, police sirens heralding unjustified searches and arrests, various states and flavors of inebriation and "Amen" responses to preaching. All these are obvious and traditional situations where a few well chosen notes can be very evocative. Err on the side of subtlety. Better to be subliminal than corny.

To make your fills a seamless part of your accompaniment, begin the line from a unison with a vocal note or comping figure. Continue the directional motion of the line or figure that you grow out of. Likewise, the end of a line can be tucked back into the texture by combining it with the beginning of the next vocal phrase or connecting to the beginning of the next accompaniment figure or bass line.

Vary your accompaniment styles and, when playing fills behind the soloist, make them predictable so they can be coped with in a musical fashion. When and if the soloist riffs or repeats any phrase, use your ear training and the information from Chapter 2 on block voicing to reinforce the vocal line.

Given time, you will develop a certain ESP with your singer which will aid in the communication of starting pitches, ritards, length of fermatas, fluctuation of dynamics and all the nuances of a great performance. A fragment of a phrase thrown into a solo or a fill can propose or dictate the next tune in the set. Duke Ellington had numerous cues like this, such as little phrases he would play to let the band know it was time for intermission (intermission riffs).

Try to incorporate some or all of these ideas as you play the following blues with your favorite singer. Play it in all keys by yourself, then experiment with transpositions in rehearsal. There's a phrase provided at the end to show how you might bring it around to the top again for an additional verse or verses.

PHOTO • IRV STEINBERG/COURTESY OF STARFILE, INC.

Duke Ellington *(on right) and* ***Count Basie*** *are cornerstones of American jazz music. They fronted brilliant big bands in the 1940s, '50s and '60s. Both were pianists of considerable skill with a solid grounding in the blues.*

THE PERFECT BLUES

Track 29

CHAPTER 7

Chicago/Delta Blues

BACKGROUND

The massive migration of Southern Blacks to the north, beginning with World War I and continuing through the early 1970s, brought the Delta blues to urban centers, most notably Chicago. This transplanted blues had already changed considerably when Muddy Waters arrived in Chicago in 1943, and would change even more as Waters and others amplified their instruments to compete with noisy urban environments. Soon after arriving, Waters worked with piano players Memphis Slim and Sunnyland Slim. Later, he hired Otis Spann. Spann remained Waters' pianist for most of his career. Some other noted Chicago Blues pianists were Big Maceo (who worked with Tampa Red, replacing Tom Dorsey) and Little Brother Montgomery.

This new urban blues was influenced by jazz and later by Motown soul. Bass lines became more independent and prominent, horn sections were added and the presentation became more polished—sometimes even including uniforms and dance steps. Rather than being based on a repeated guitar or left-hand piano figure, a blues was more likely to be based on a repeated riff or riff-like bass figure. Jazz-style solos by horn players, guitar players and keyboardists began to be featured between vocal choruses. As a result of playing more with rhythm sections, piano players began using their left hands less. The minor blues scale became more prevalent, as did the shuffle feel with swung eighth notes. The music became more urgent and generally darker. Amplification allowed guitar players to draw Banshee shrieks out of bent strings which would have otherwise been barely audible. This, too, changed the style of playing. The old down-home styles were still used, but less frequently and recast in this more modern style. Different rural strains were combined in new and unusual ways because of the widespread roots of the migration, and a freer spirit of experimentation resulted in interesting hybrids. New Orleans influences, Latin and jump blues played by the big bands all had an impact.

The normal size of a working band also changed. The typical Delta blues ensemble ranged from a single guitar player to a piano duo or trio with bass and/or guitar. There might also be a violinist or harmonica player. Muddy Waters' band with two (and sometimes three) guitars, harmonica, piano, bass and drums became the model for all Chicago blues bands. The role of the piano player changed from providing fills and a foundation in the left hand to playing fills in free exchanges with the vocalist and the other musicians in the band.

STRUCTURE

The classic Chicago blues fill is an ascending segment of the blues scale, a repeated note, tremolo diad, tremolo octave or repeated scale segment, then a descending blues scale release. The starting point in the scale, length of scale and number of repetitions of the arrival point are all variable. The repetitions almost always reinforce the triplet-eighth pulse, although occasionally a player may play sixteenth notes or quarter-note triplets for a change of feel. Typically, while one player sounds the repeated notes or ostinato in the middle of the phrase, the other musicians will superimpose their own phrases of shorter length. The resulting structure becomes: vocal phrase; primary fill; subsidiary fills inside the primary fill; end of the primary fill.

Chicago Blues Fills

Measure:	1	2	3	4	5	6
Solo Phrase	VOCAL				VOCAL	
Primary fill						
Subsidiary fill						
Measure:	**7**	**8**	**9**	**10**	**11**	**12**
Solo Phrase			VOCAL		Turnaround..............................	
Primary fill						
Subsidiary fill						

The roles are not rigid and the overall texture is very *contrapuntal* (more than one melody at a time). Usually, no one really plays chords. However, someone is almost always sustaining a note or a tremolo so that the effect isn't too thin. If the vocal phrase is *compound* (built from sub-phrases) fills are inserted between the sub-phrases, often split between two different instruments.

PHOTO • COURTESY OF INSTITUTE OF JAZZ STUDIES

***Otis Spann** is considered by many to be the greatest blues ensemble pianist ever. In 1952, Otis Spann was introduced to Muddy Waters by Len Chess, and joined Muddy in what would become a history-making band. Spann's solid, powerful playing style was derived in large part from Maceo Merriweather, who was on the Chicago scene before him. But Otis's unique contribution to the art was in finding the perfect way to make his bold sounds enhance but never intrude upon the new sounds of the Chicago blues.*

BASS LINES

In this book, everything should be played with a swing feel unless marked "*Straight 8ths*."

The recommended tempo for all the examples on this page is ♩= 120.

The following examples typify how bass figures were transformed. Here is a familiar bass figure:

In Chicago style, this common shuffle bass line is played without *double stops* (two notes played simultaneously by one player).

Likewise, the *old-timey* two-beat of Delta blues....

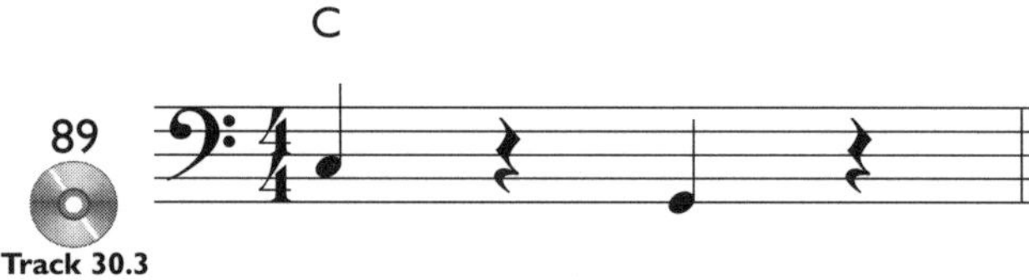

...might become this:

or this:

The Motown influence is apparent in bass lines such as these:

INTROS AND ENDINGS

Most endings in Chicago blues are variations on a final turnaround on the second half of the second beat of bar 12. Introductions are another story, forming almost a compendium of ways to start a blues.

With the expanded role of improvisation, an instrumental solo one chorus or more in length might precede the entrance of the singer. Partial choruses starting in bar 9 or bar 5 are also common, and the traditional half-cadence turnaround (ending on the V7 chord) also makes frequent appearances, usually decorated with improvisation. Sometimes, an open vamp on the I chord is used and, if the blues is based on a riff, a few repetitions of the riff make an adequate intro. Also not uncommon is starting with no introduction. At the other extreme, a *cadenza* (an unaccompanied solo passage) before the rest of the band enters is sometimes used—from a few pick-up notes in length to an entire verse. This first chorus is sometimes played *stop time*. In stop time, punctuations of the tonic chord or statements of a riff separate the vocal or instrumental phrases starting in bar 5, bar 9 or at the turnaround.

Punctuating the Tonic in Stop Time

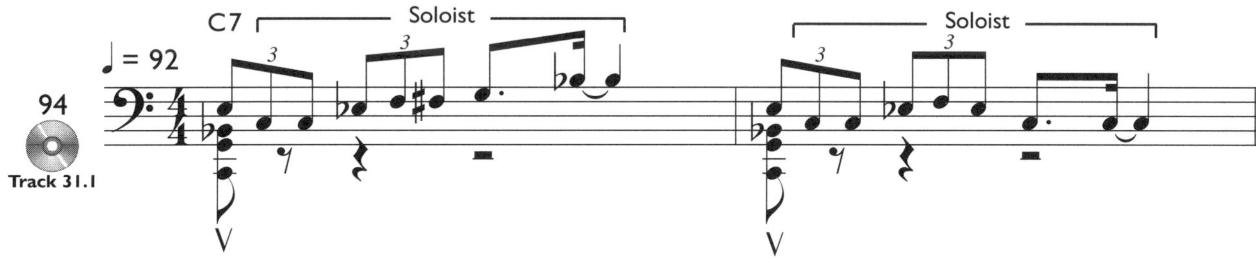

Use of a Riff in Stop Time

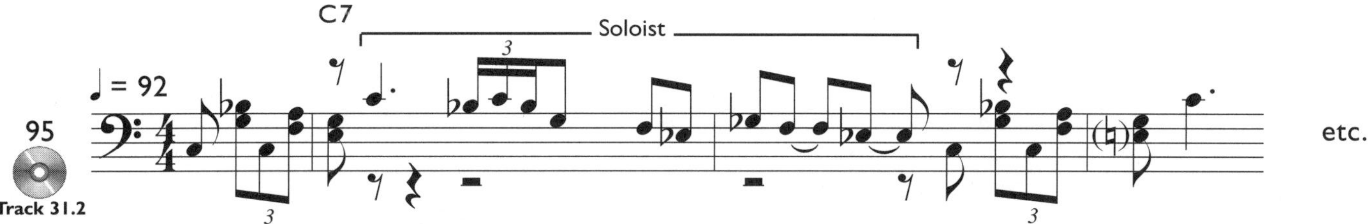

THE STYLES OF SPANN AND MONTGOMERY

Below is a piece in the style of Otis Spann. Except where indicated (by the "L.H." marking), the left hand can play chord voicings in the comping register as a jazz pianist would.

If you have the CD that is available for this book, leave the bass line to the bass player or better yet, find yourself a bass player (a good bass figure is shown at the end of the piece).

WORKIN' THE HAND SPANN BLUES

Track 32

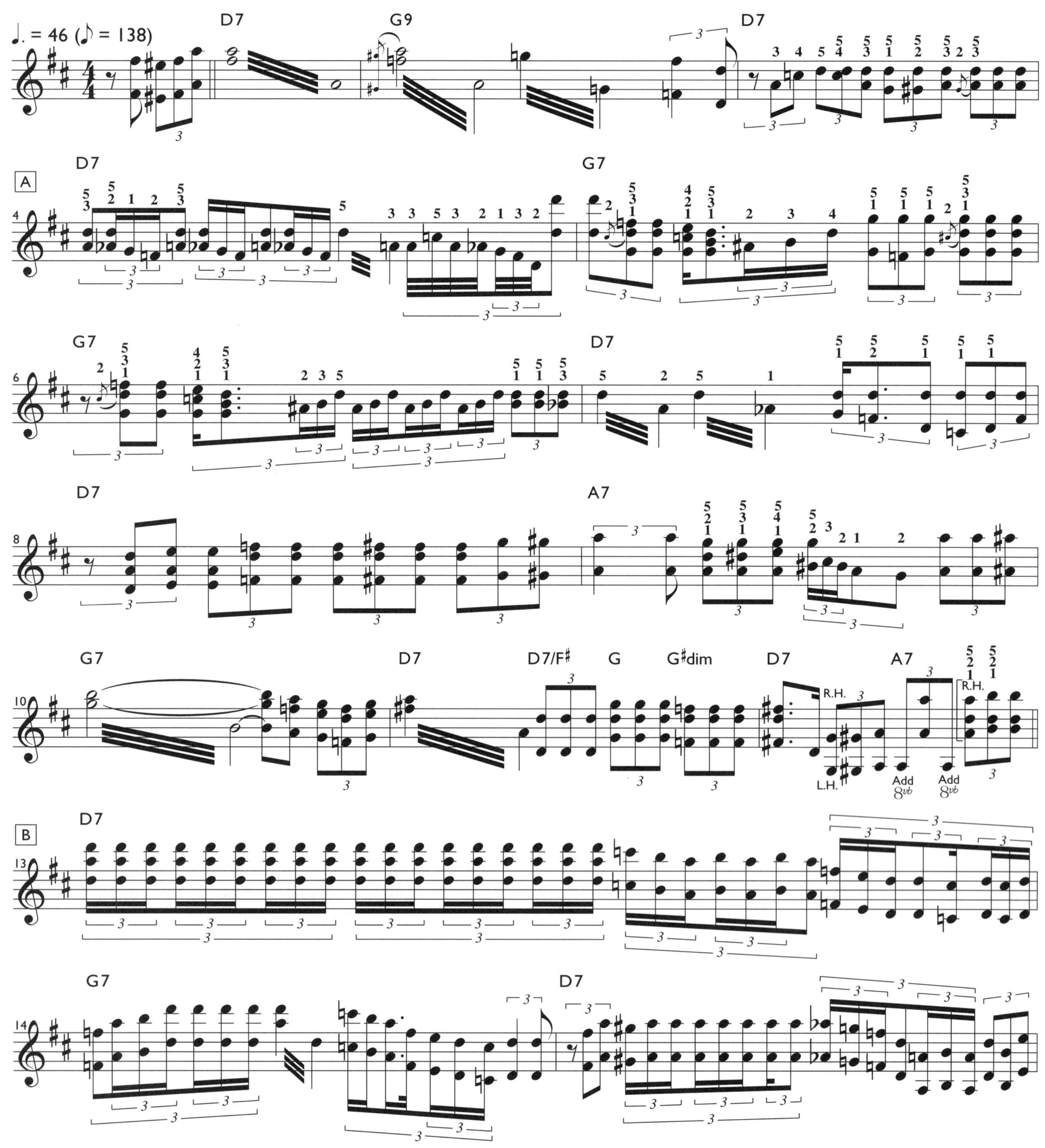

Here is the suggested bass figure for this tune.

The playing of Eurreal "Little Brother" Montgomery was influenced by jazz. He led a swing band in the 1930s in Mississippi but became a fixture of the Chicago blues scene. This piano solo incorporates some of the elements of his style.

YOUR BROTHER'S KEEPER BLUES

D♭7 C7 B7 B♭7 B7 C7 D♭7 A♭7
E♭7 (A♭/E♭) A♭7 A♭dim D♭min7/A♭ A♭
A♭dim7 A♭7
E♭7 A♭

CHAPTER 8

New Orleans R&B

MUSICAL GUMBO

In this book, everything should be played with a swing feel unless marked "*Straight 8ths*."

New Orleans, renowned as the birthplace of jazz, was the intersection of five major cultures: African, French, Spanish, Celtic and American Indian. Traces of these influences are apparent in New Orleans blues.

New Orleans R&B shares with jazz the African features of call and response, African rhythms and the blues scale used over European harmonies (first fused in the spiritual Protestant hymns sung in an African style—probably beginning in the earliest days of slavery). Unlike Chicago-style blues, the major forms of the blues scale predominate in New Orleans blues.

The French and Spanish influences are apparent in the preference for eight-bar blues and thirty-two-bar song form in New Orleans blues. This is a remnant of the dance music which the Europeans brought with them. The biggest influence, however, comes through the *Contredanse,* in particular the *Cinque,* an Africanization of a European dance form with a five-note rhythm:

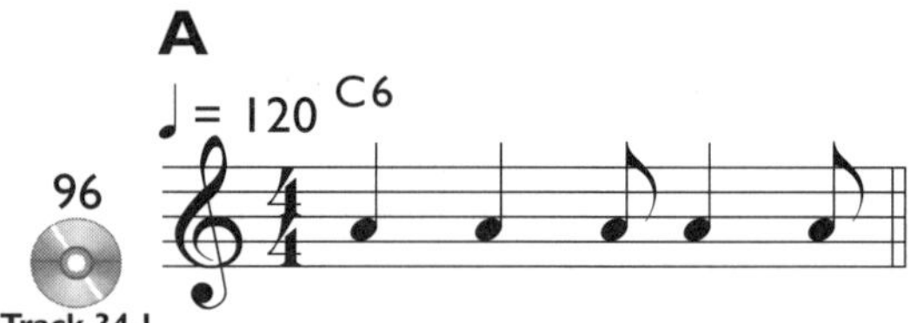

The so called *second line*, almost always present in New Orleans music, is the *clavé* rhythm. To the present day, rock'n'roll and R&B are still underpinned by the clave.

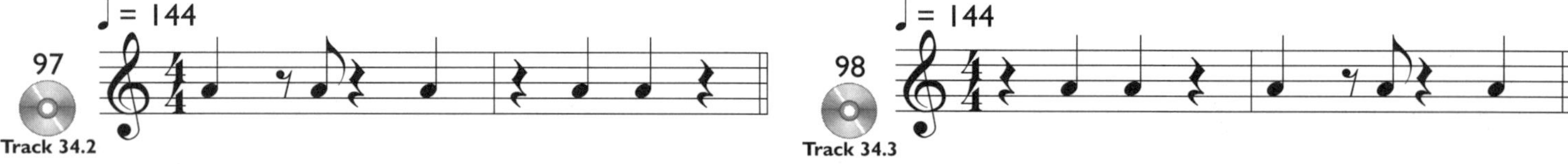

Like gumbo, a New Orleans dish that contains a little bit of everything at hand, music in New Orleans is a mixture of ragtime, Dixieland jazz, Cajun (French Acadian), Zydeco, rhumba, mambo, Calypso, flamenco, Celtic jigs and reels and Irish ballads.

New Orleans blues reflects its proximity to and shared history with all these styles.

LONGHAIR BLUES

In *Intermediate Blues Keyboard,* you were introduced to the reputation and musical style of Roy Byrd, A.K.A Professor Longhair. Two of his influences were Sullivan Rock and Robert Bertrand ("Kid Stormy Weather"), and he is regarded as a forefather of Mac Rebennack ("Dr. John"), Allan Toussaint, James Booker, Huey "Piano" Smith, Fats Domino, Harry Connick, Jr. and many others. Collecting and studying recordings of these artists is highly recommended.

Right-hand figures in the New Orleans piano style tend towards a high degree of ornamentation and much use of repeated short figures. These are both melodic groove figures designed to propel the feel and the time. One of Professor Longhair's pet phrases is an arpeggio or pentatonic scale, usually descending, with a single sixteenth-note triplet turn.

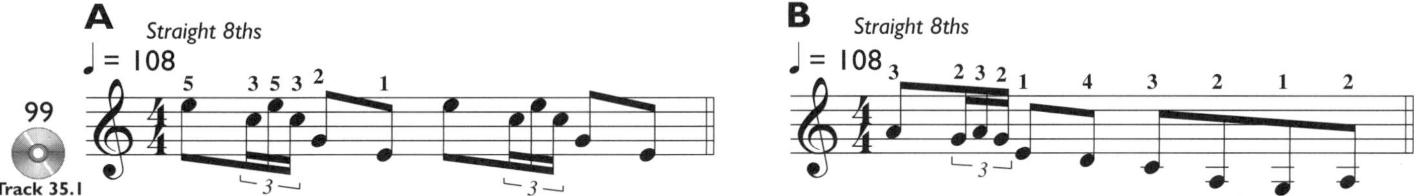

Figures with double stops moving in parallel motion and chromatic passing tones in the lower voice are common.

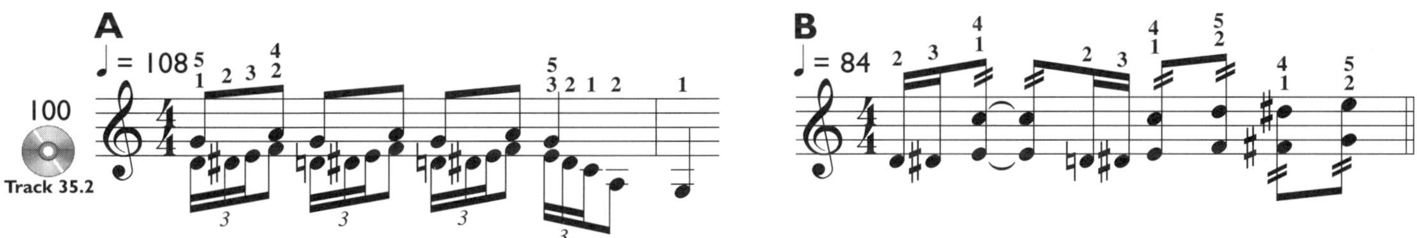

Tremolos are common, but more often as the beginnings or ends of phrases, unlike Chicago blues where they appear more frequently at the peaks.

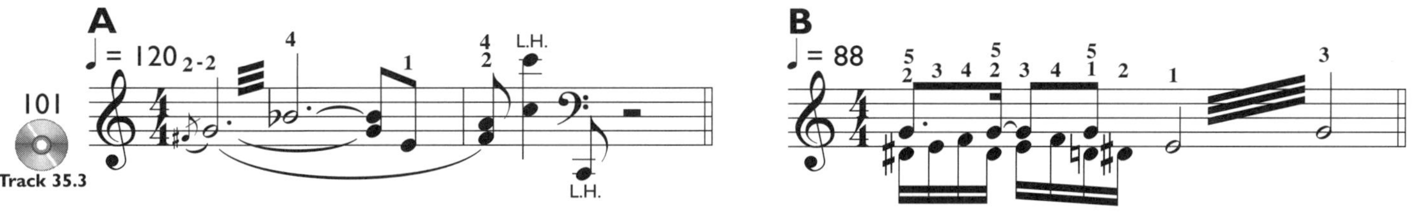

Humorous, quotation-like interjections seeming to come from completely different styles and unrelated tunes are a favorite device. This is another reflection on the musical diversity of the region.

Since the emphasis is on feel rather than on virtuosity, right-hand figures that merely outline the harmony or divide the chord into two parts, creating a cross-rhythmic pulse, are abundant.

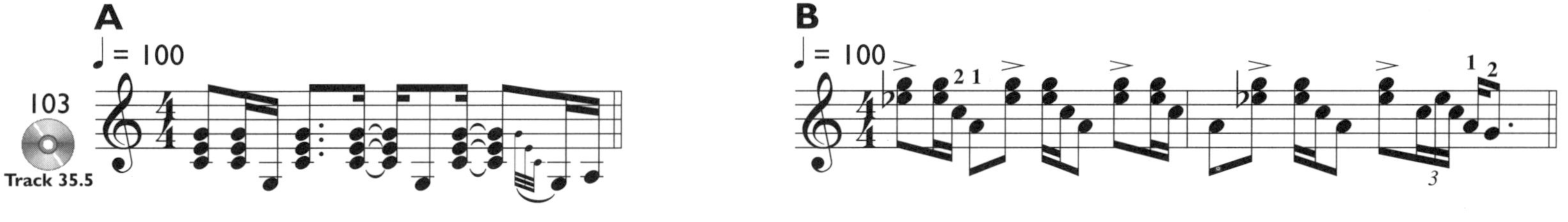

NEW ORLEANS ACCOMPANIMENT STYLES

A typical New Orleans tune is as recognizable by its feel and accompaniment as it is by its melodic and lyrical content. Below is a list of just a few possibilities. You will have to augment this list through your continued listening studies.

1. The always-present dotted-quarter note bass line (the three-note part of the clavé), with its myriad variations, straight or swung, with the right hand playing eighth notes, quarter notes or any number of groove figures.

2. The walking bass in quarter notes (in the boogie-woogie style, not a free walking line). This can be straight or swung, with right-hand chords on the off-beats. (The bass line often has broken octaves, since that is a similar effect to playing chords on the off-beats.)

3. Decoration of the clave in the right hand over a walking bass (repeated figure) or divided between the two hands.

4. Stride, in its pure form, makes many appearances. It also appears with the backbeat doubled in a swing eighth feel, reflecting a West Indian influence.

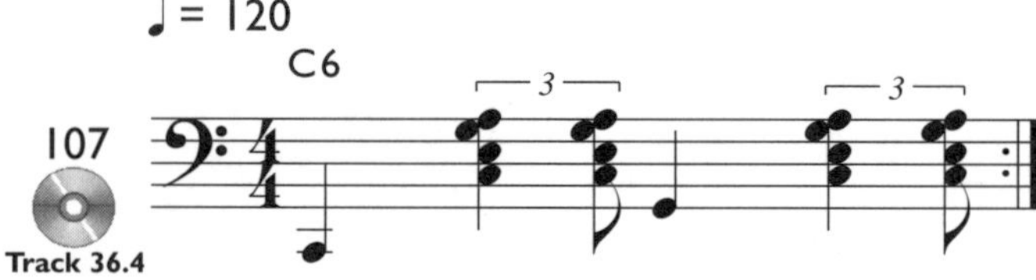

5. In Chapter 4, we introduced the concept of bass notes alternating with chords in a rudimental pattern in the style of James Booker. This also occurs in quarter notes as an alternative to stride.

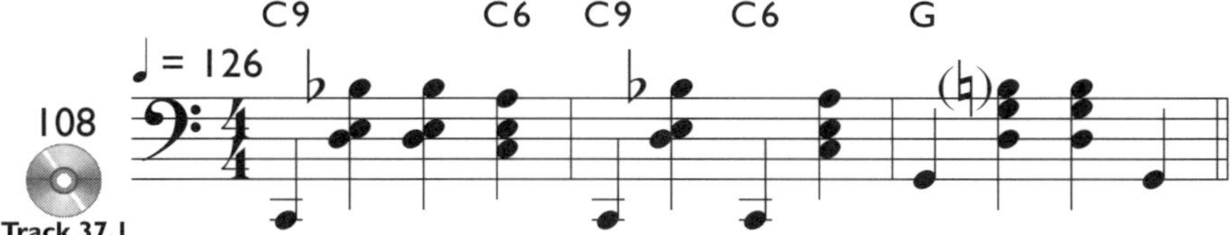

6. Another James Booker favorite is this one bar repeated left-hand rhythm.

7. Shuffle-type bass lines, of a type borrowed from Chicago blues, are sometimes used as are some classic boogie-woogie broken-octave figures.

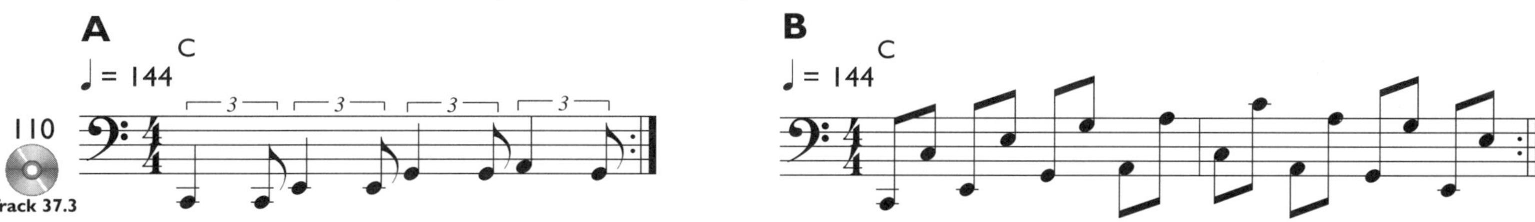

8. The clavé rhythm is sometimes played as a double-time riff over either a walking line or the dotted-quarter rhythm variations.

9. Many bass lines are borrowed from R&B and 1950s rock'n'roll:

When looking for recordings of Alan Toussaint, called by some "The Bach of New Orleans," you will find some early recordings under the name *Tousan*. The following piece is in the style of those early recordings, which already exhibit the clarity of form and virtuosic simplicity that are featured in his work as a major producer of R&B.

ODE: TOUSAN—ITY BLUES

B
E7
A7
E7
B7
A7
E7
B7
D.S. al Coda
Coda
B7
E
B7 E

James Booker was probably the New Orleans pianist most respected by his peers. Booker was a musical genius of the first order. Classically trained, he played Chopin from memory at a very early age, and it is said he could play solos that he heard for the first time *backwards*. This title comes from something he was quoted as saying while sailing near the end of his life.

JAMMIN' WITH THE WIND

Emin
2.4.
Emin
Repeat to A
Emin B7/F♯ Emin/G G♯dim A A♯dim E/B
rit.
1st time, continue to B
On D.S., skip to D.C al Fine
♩ = 144
B
8va
E
B7
(8va)
B7
E7
B7/F♯
Play 4 times
1st & 4th times as written
2nd & 3rd times improvise RH
Play 4 times
(8va)
B7
B7
ritard
loco
Repeat ad lib.
ritard
D.S.

CHAPTER 9

Burnin', Layin' Back and Bringin' It All Home

By now you know that rhythmic content in the blues is paramount. Mainstream artists stay very close to a handful of chord progressions, a few scales, even fewer meters and the subject matter of the lyrics stays within fairly narrow confines. Every tune will have one or two fresh devices used to distinguish it from others, but the real creative energy is expended inventing a unique rhythmic feel and using signature or spontaneously composed rhythmic devices in solos.

To use a single rhythmic value through an entire solo, while possible, would be not be in the style. It would not engage the listener as intensely as moving from one rhythmic level to another. Think of the available rhythmic values, from the smallest subdivision to the longest note you can conceive of playing. Now make a list of these rhythmic values, from sixteenth-note triplets or thirty-second notes as the fastest to tied whole notes. Think of this list as being your "scale" of rhythmic values.

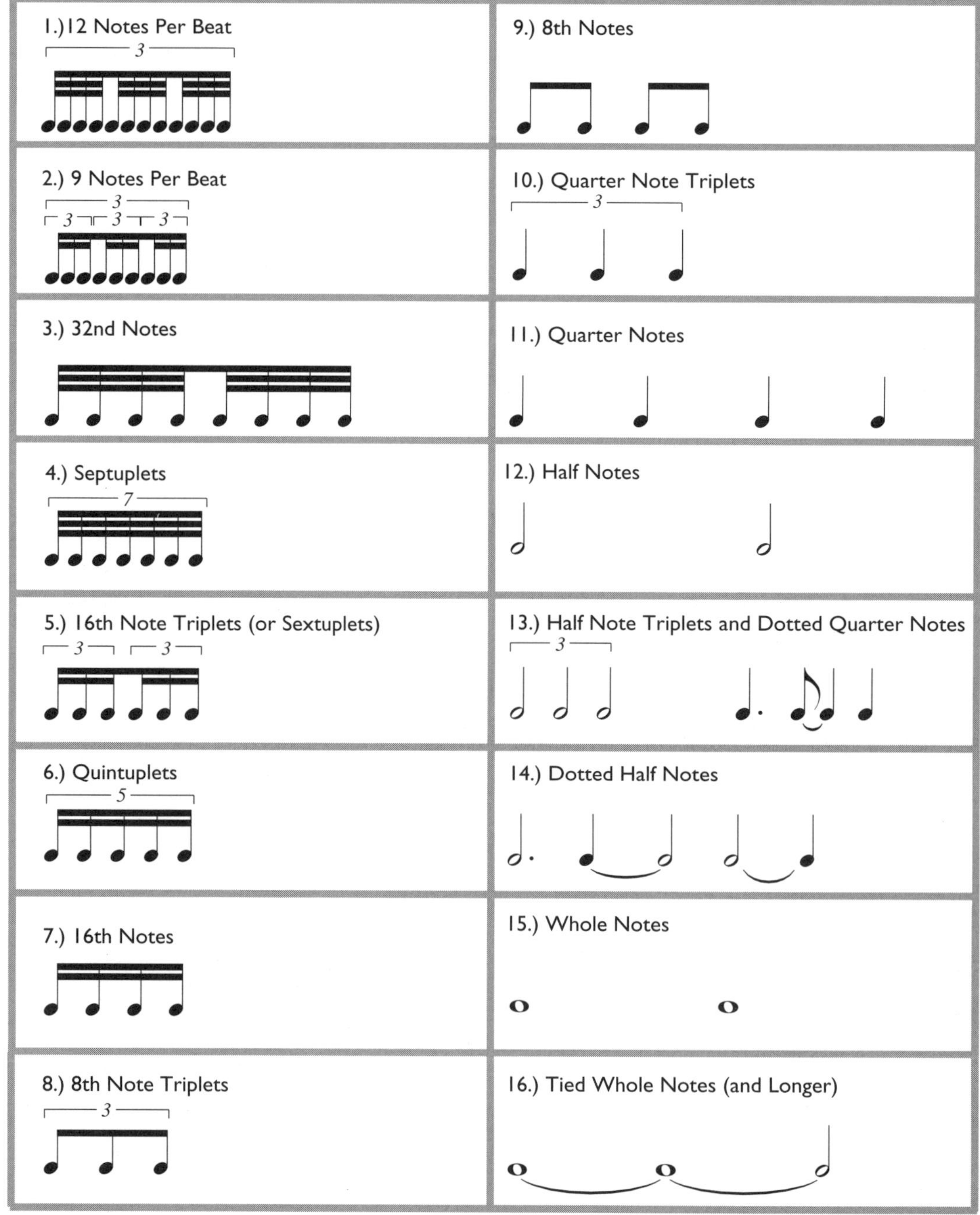

BURNIN'

Each of the rhythmic values has a feel that is affected by the pulse of the meter in the rhythm section underneath it. If the rhythm in your solo makes a polyrhythm (page 53) when paired with the meter of the rhythm section, the result is a gain of energy and interest. This is because the two rhythms will make a larger number of attacks in different places within the bar and because of the division of the listener's attention between the two rhythmic streams.

As typified by the classic Chicago blues phrase you learned in Chapter 7, one often-used rhythmic contour is moving from smaller subdivisions (the low end of our "scale") to larger values in mid-phrase and back at phrase end. The effect of this is an increase in emotional tension followed by a release. If the longer notes are tremolos, one might consider this to be movement from slightly larger values to the smaller values in the tremolo or trill.

The opposite shape is also typical—moving from large note values to faster movement in the phrase giving an effect called *burning* or *wailing* mid-flight.

It is common practice to use smaller subdivisions at phrase beginnings and endings. This results in several effects:

- The soloist seems to have an inexhaustible supply of ideas and is trying to get as many as possible out in a single breath.

- The interest level is intensified just before the next breath or pause is taken.

- The end of the phrase seems much less final, and the motion is better sustained from one phrase to the next because the actual end point is more difficult to discern.

- Every phrase has greater tension at the center, less at the ends.

- The illusion of *riding* on top of the rhythm section is enhanced by seeming to tumble and having to regain one's equilibrium.

Some movement in the "Scale of Rhythmic Values" is a traditional part of the blues language. For instance, beginning a line with an ascending scale in quarter-note triplets, usually leaving out the first one or more notes and continuing with either faster or slower movement, is associated with *soulfulness*, and the quarter-note triplets call attention to the beginning of the phrase. Another example would be an *ostinato* figure (a repeated figure) in faster values as the peak of a phrase. And as a final example, the tried-and-true tactic of beginning with large note values, played so as to give the feeling of mass, moving gradually to smaller note values as the solo progresses for that speedy, macho, muscular, "leave 'em drenched in their own sweat" climax.

***James P. Johnson** became known as the father of stride piano. In the 1920s his popularity flourished. He wrote many piano pieces, songs and Broadway shows.*

PHOTO • COURTESY OF INSTITUTE OF JAZZ STUDIES

LAYIN' BACK

To get the full effect of a slow blues, motion on the "Scale of Rhythmic Values" must be downward, from smaller to larger note values, usually between adjacent levels. The line being played this way must have a logical and predictable sense of motion. The predictability of the line is what allows the soloist to pull the audience onto a separate rhythmic plane, slower than that of the rhythm section. This can be done by simply slowing the end of a phrase so it's extended past the bar line.

In this book, everything should be played with a swing feel unless marked "*Straight 8ths.*"

Or, totally disregard the band's tempo and grind to a halt at the end of a solo.

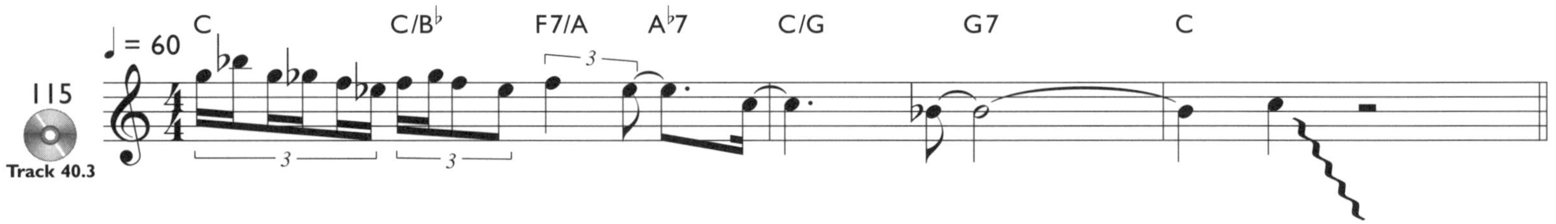

Extremely slow blues tempos represent a plane of reality far removed from the tempo of modern life. The soloist who can ride the feel comfortably and bring the listener into that plane is a master of the art of the blues.

PHOTO • COURTESY OF INSTITUTE OF JAZZ STUDIES

Roosevelt "The Honeydripper" Sykes, *born in 1906, was equally gifted as a blues pianist, songwriter and singer. He frequently sang while he played, but also accompanied many great blues vocalists. Roosevelt began his career in St. Louis at the age of 14, ran away to play in barrelhouses in Mississippi and Louisiana when he was 15, and made his first recording for Okeh records in New York at the age of 23. He later spent a great deal of time in Chicago where he was an integral part of the Chicago blues scene, influencing many young pianists, especially Memphis Slim. Listen to blues by Roosevelt "The Honeydripper" Sykes on Smithsonian/Folkways recordings for some incredible playing.*

BRINGIN' IT ALL HOME

A further use for slowing over the time—moving sequentially downward in our "Scale of Rhythmic Values"—is to signal that the end of your solo or the tune is near. These cues can be quite subtle or obvious, reversing the process discussed in the *Burnin'* section. That is to say, the fast movement of solos and melody can give way to increasingly slower note values. This creates the illusion that the quick, seemingly easy movement in the flight of the tune had so much momentum that it required industrial strength muscle to stop it. Simply playing a cliché turnaround after a long solo is a perfect way to stop this momentum and, along with plain old shoe familiarity, at least part of the reason the traditional final cadence is so satisfying.

Another way of delaying the end of the tune is the *tag*. A basic blues tag is done by remaining on the tonic in bars 11 and 12, and then returning to bar 9 to repeat the final four bars, thus increasing the importance and inevitability of the final turnaround. If you are playing in a band, this may have to be worked out in advance.

If you are using ii7 and V7 in bars 9 and 10, a further possibility is the "*really mean it*" ending. This is a deceptive cadence to the iii7 chord (or III7, making it a *secondary dominant*—dominant of the VI). Or, you can play a deceptive cadence to the ♭VII7, the tritone substitute for III7. In either case, you then play a cycle of 5ths back to the tonic (ii-V-I). In a more jazz-oriented context, ♭iii7 and ♭VI7 can be substituted for iii7 and VI7.

Choose any one of these three...

Measure:	9	10	11	12
Possible Harmonies:	**V7**	**IV7**	**I**	**I**
	ii7	**V7**	**III7 or ♭VII7**	**VI7**
	ii7	**V7**	**♭iii7**	**♭VI7**

...followed by a tag:

Measure:	9	10	11	12
Possible Harmonies:	**V7**	**IV7**	**I IV**	**I V7 I**
	ii7	**V7**	**I IV**	**I V7 I**

One sometimes hears the III7 – VII7 – ii7 –V7 section of the progression repeated three times. Occasionally, as Claire Fischer, the West Coast keyboard master and composer once said, it can become "... one of those tunes where the coda goes on to become a separate tune."

In this piano solo, which uses some of the ideas we just introduced, your mission—should you accept it—is to write your own melody over this left-hand figure. Use the melody provided here as inspiration. Play the second chorus over this bass line. Remember, there are twelve eighth notes in the bar.

> If you are playing along with the CD that is available for this book, take a solo during the repeat of the [A] section.

BLUES FOR HEAVY ROTATION

Track 41

♩. = 54

Amin · Dmin/C · Dmin7 · C

1st time play fills

Play 2nd time only

[A]

Amin · Dmin/C · Dmin7 · C

Amin · Dmin/C · Dmin7

Dmin7 · F · Dmin

G7
F
Dmin
C
Amin
Emin/D
Emin7
F/E♭
F7
Emin7
C
To Coda
B 2nd Chorus
Amin
Dmin
Dmin
Amin
Dmin
Dmin
G9
Dmin
Amin
Emin
F/E♭
F7
Emin7
C
D.S. al Coda
Amin
Amin/C
Dmin7
D♯dim7
E
Amin
Coda
Right hand improvise
R.H.
L.H.

CHAPTER 10

Boogie-Woogie

When the barrelhouse pianists of the logging camps in the Southern United States followed the northward migration, their music morphed into a more sophisticated, urban music which came to be known as boogie-woogie. You have already been introduced to Jimmy Yancey and Clarence "Pine Top" Smith. Some other names associated with the style are Pete Johnson, Albert Ammons, Cow Cow Davenport, Hershal Thomas and Meade "Lux" Lewis.

Clarence Smith's *Pine Top Boogie* was the first major boogie-woogie hit in 1928, and Tommy Dorsey's version of the tune (1938) began the second wave of popularity which lasted through World War II, peaking with *Boogie-Woogie Bugle Boy* by the Andrews Sisters.

BASS LINES

The essential element in boogie-woogie is the left-hand bass ostinato (examples 116, 118-121) comprised of eight eighth notes (as codified by the pop hit, *Beat Me, Daddy, Eight to the Bar* by Will Bradley). Generally, some kind of double melodic line is present or implied. Broken octaves are often a feature, as well. Right-hand material is often rhythmic rather than melodic. When it is melodic, it is relatively simple and repetitive, designed to create cross rhythms and syncopations. Chord progressions in boogie-woogie are usually very basic, omitting the turn-around in bars 11 and 12, remaining on the I chord, and seldom using the IV chord in bar 2. In bars 9 and 10, iimin7 to V7 and V7 to IV7 are common, but of equal or greater frequency is remaining on the V chord through both bars.

> In this book, everything should be played with a swing feel unless marked "*Straight 8ths*."

Here is an abbreviated catalog of left- and right-hand boogie-woogie figures.

In the style of the left-hand part of *Honky Tonk Train Blues* by Meade "Lux" Lewis:

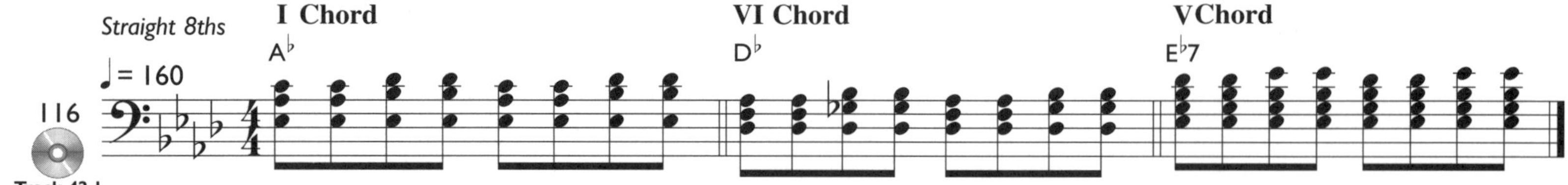

Also in the style of *Honky Tonk Train Blues*, this is an interesting example of the double melodic line in the right hand.

Both Albert Ammons and Meade "Lux" Lewis sometimes use a "block voice" bass line.

= Roll the chord.

Here is another left-hand figure in the style of Albert Ammons' *Boogie-Woogie Stomp.*

Straight 8ths

Here is a bass line in the style of Pete Johnson's *Roll Em' Pete*, also called *Climbin' and Screamin'*.

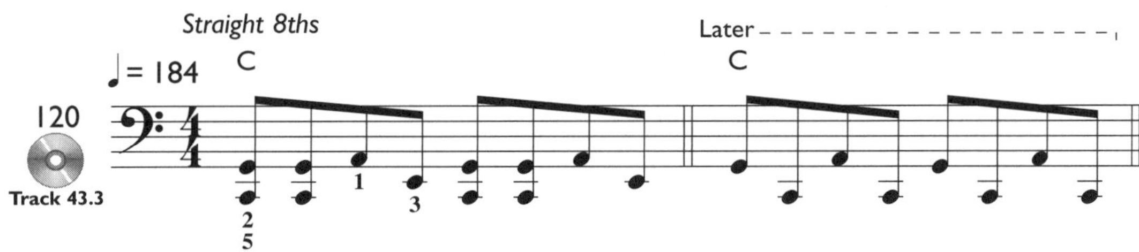

Here are two left-hand figures in the style of James P. Johnson.

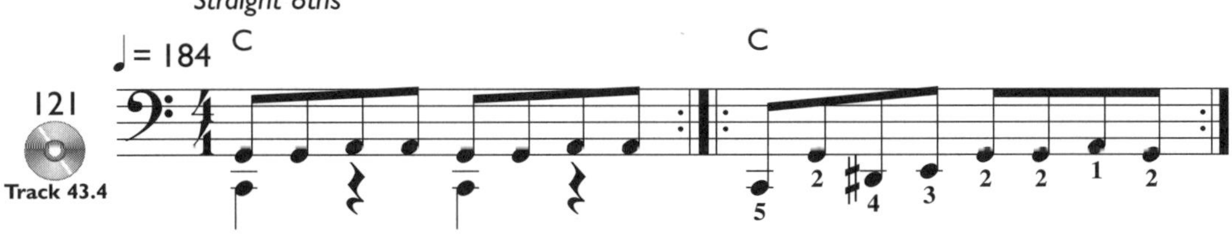

MOTIFS

Here is a challenge for you. Meade "Lux" Lewis recorded an amazing piece called *Variations on a Theme, Part I – 19 Ways of Playing a Chorus* (on harpsichord!). The chord progression is the simplest possible, using the V chord in bars 9 and 10 and the I chord in bars 11 and 12. Below is a list of nineteen motifs in the style of those he used to develop each chorus. See if you can create a chorus using each. After you have done this, compare your results with Lewis'. (The CD is "Blue Boogie, Boogie-woogie, Stride and the Piano Blues," on Bluenote CPD 7990992.)

BASS LINE:

MOTIFS:

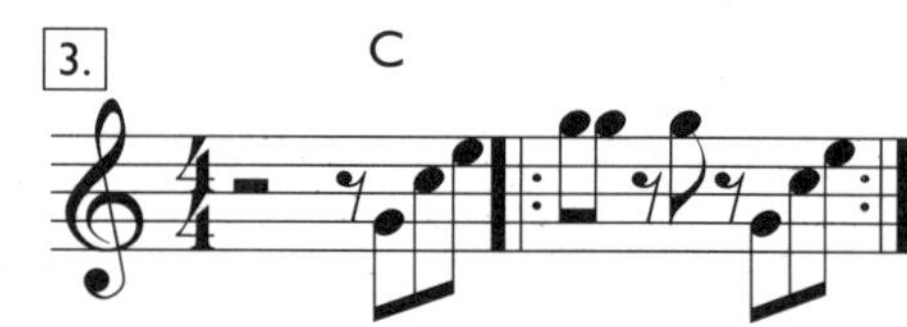

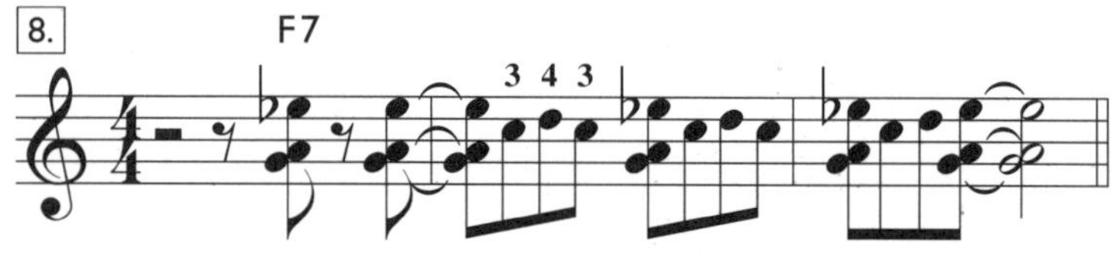

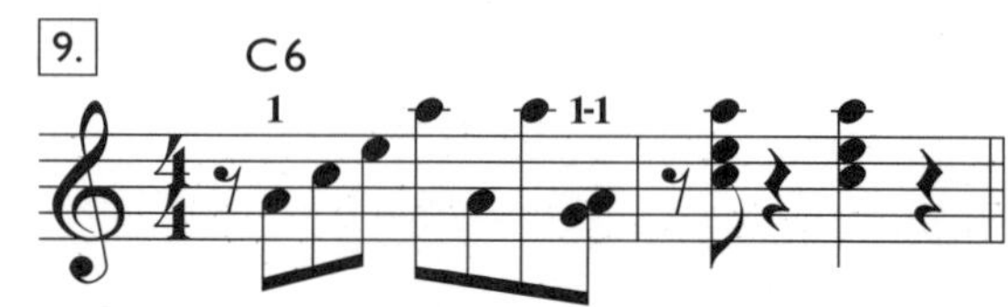

10.
C6

11.
C

12.
C

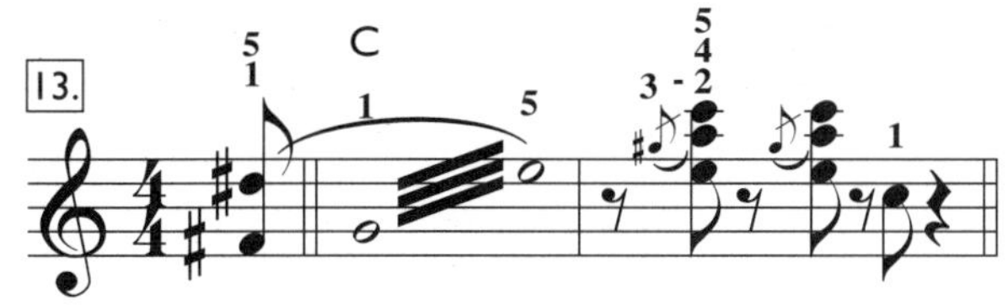
13.
C

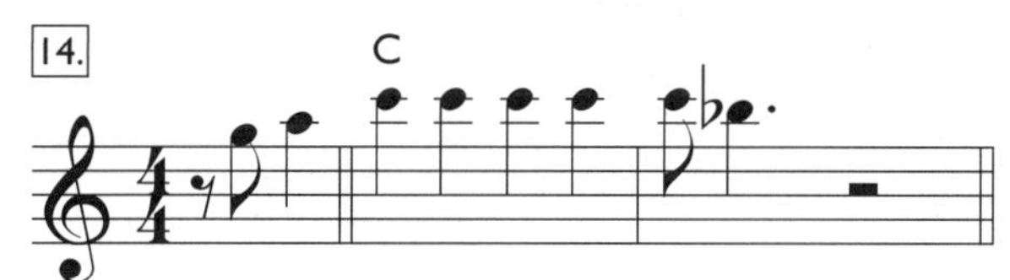
14.
C

15.
C
C9

16.
C

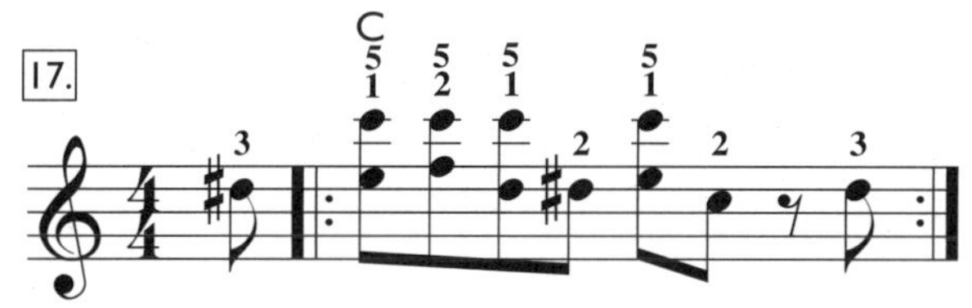
17.
C

18.
C

19.
C
C9

This piece uses the boogie-woogie style combined with more contemporary jazz harmonies such as the ♯9. It uses a device called *octave displacement* —putting one note in a line an octave higher or lower, either in the left hand and/or the right hand. For instance, look at the bass line in the second half of bar 3. The A in the line F♯, G, A is displaced up one octave.

THE STAR BOOGIE

Track 44

A♭/E♭
E♭
D♭/E♭
E♭/F
A♭/E♭
E♭
D♭/E♭
B/D♭
G/A
B♭/C
E/G♭
C/D
A♭/B♭
B/D♭
F/G
G♭/A♭
G/A
A♭/B♭
BMaj7
C7,♯9
C
F7
C7,♯9
Play 3 times
F7
C7,♯9
F7/C
Play 4 times
C7,♯9
F7
C
D
2nd time two octaves lower
*Play 2nd time only
C7
E
To Coda
C7
Play 6 times
1st & 2nd times as written
3rd, 4th & 5th times improvise R.H.
6th time as written
Then D.S. al Coda
Coda
C

CHAPTER 11

Gospel

BACKGROUND

As the chanel for African musical influence in America, the Black church is the source of almost all our popular musical styles. From as early as 1750, there are reports of slaves singing Protestant hymns in a specialized way complete with descriptions of call and response in the form of *lining out* (chanting or singing a line sometimes using a different melody than the hymn being performed). This style of singing spread throughout the U.S. with the various "awakenings" and "revivals" of the late 1800s and early 1900s, taking root most strongly in the South. The Baptist, Methodist and Pentecostal churches all developed their own idiomatic strains, with the Pentecostal's being the most uninhibited expression, including percussion instruments, stamping, clapping and shouting. In the early 1900s, the Jubilee Quartet, which was four male voices singing a'capella, became the dominant Gospel performing group.

One of the first Gospel pianists and singers was Arizona Dranes. She set the classic Gospel accompaniment style with her combination of Protestant hymn harmony, ragtime two-beat and elements of barrelhouse piano. She was also one of the first to record that stylized triplet feel which, by the 1950s, had become the familiar $\frac{12}{8}$.

In Chapter 7, you were introduced to Thomas A. Dorsey who, with Hudson Whittaker (Tampa Red), had several non-religious chart hits. After a nervous break-down, Dorsey returned to Gospel music. Previously he had lived a "double life." Even his parents didn't know of his career playing "the Devil's music." He became known as the father of Gospel music.

Another sacred keyboardist who had a career in secular music was Kenneth Morris, who first used the Hammond organ in Gospel music. The piano and Hammond together are considered the perfect accompaniment in Gospel circles. Both Dorsey and Morris were prolific composers and became important publishers in the Gospel field as well.

Some other early pianists and organists who deserve mention are:

Estelle Allen
Mildred Falls
Evelyn Gay
Gwendolyn Cooper Lightener

All four of these artists were pianists for Mahalia Jackson, the New Orleans-based gospel singer, at one time or another. Jackson was a strictly spiritual singer (she would not perform in clubs) and was world famous until her death in 1972. Her first hit was *Lift Every Voice And Sing* in 1956. She recorded with Duke Ellington, sang for presidents and performed at many of Martin Luther King's appearances.

In the 1950s, pianists were so integral to the music that their names were often included in the group's name. Some important players of this time were:

Curtis Dublin, whose style incorporated elements of jazz.

Herbert Pickard

Roberta Martin, who was the pianist for Thomas Dorsey's Gospel choir at the Pilgrim Baptist Church and later, an important exponent of Gospel music with her group, the Roberta Martin Singers.

Clara Ward of the Clara Ward Singers.

The third wave of Gospel keyboardists includes such artists as:

Doris Akers, a composer, director and arranger who started as a singer in the *Sally Martin Singers*. Martin was an associate of Thomas Dorsey.

"Professor" Alex Bradford

James Cleveland, a composer and arranger of prodigious ability who directed and coached many prominent Gospel groups and was an architect of the modern Gospel sound.

Jessy Dixon

James Herndon

Raymond Rasberry

Lawrence Roberts

Charles Taylor

Gospel music has always been an enormous influence on jazz artists (such as Cannonball Adderly, Oliver Nelson, Joseph Zawinul and Charles Mingus) and R&B musicians (not just Sam Cooke, Al Green and others who started in Gospel, but practically every Motown artist). Gospel music entered the Pop realm with the Edwin Hawkins crossover hit of 1969, *O Happy Day*. Many genres have been adapted for use in Gospel music, from Handel's *Messiah* (Quincy Jones) to the most current pop and R&B stylings. It has also been a tradition to write religious words to popular songs.

In this book we will touch only on the basics of "classic" Gospel. For further guidance, the prescription is a heavy dose of listening to the recordings of all the artists listed here, watching or listening to Gospel shows and/or attendance at the Pentecostal church of your choice.

THE STYLE

The first element in Gospel piano accompaniment is heavy repeated chords, usually with octave doublings in close position played in the comping register. If you have to go out of the comping register, extend it downward rather than upward. The chord is often broken into two parts and used as a groove figure, or the IV chord is inserted in the middle of the rhythmic figure for added motion. Note that gospel tunes are frequently in $\frac{3}{4}$.

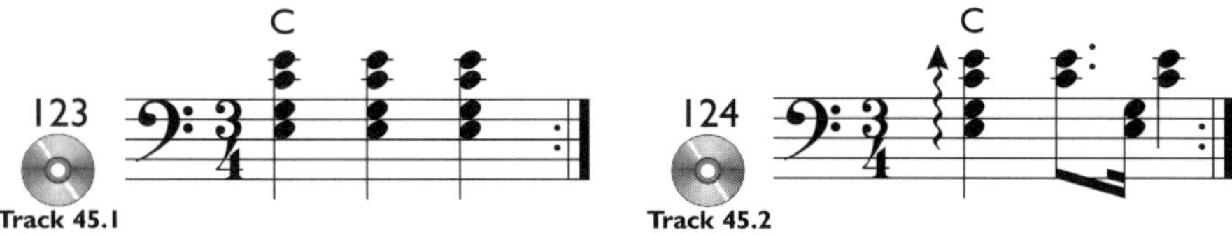

> In this book, everything should be played with a swing feel unless marked "*Straight 8ths.*"

> The recommended tempo for all the examples on this page is ♩= 84.

The second element is the bass line in octaves, usually in the lowest possible register for weight, with diatonic or chromatic sweeps leading into each new chord root.

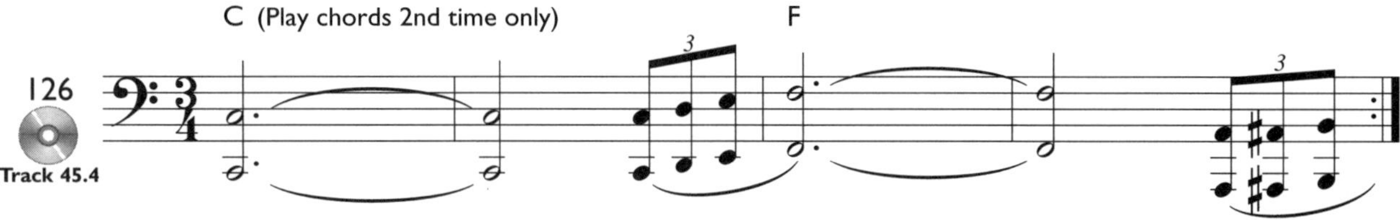

The third element is fills, which can be in the bass register as well as the treble, and are often in octaves, although single-note runs are also frequent. These runs usually have just a handful of notes. Pentatonic rather than diatonic scales prevail.

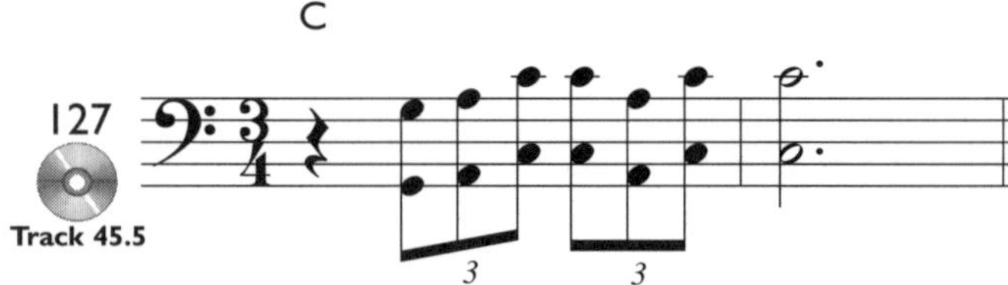

The recommended tempo for all the examples on this page is ♩= 84.

Cadences are typically *plagal* (I – IV – I) or iimin7 – V7 with the bass line harmonized (iimin7 – iiimin7 – IV — ♯ivdim – V).

Another common harmonic structure borrowed from European music via the Protestant hymnal is I – iimin7 – I – IV or IV – I– iimin7 – I.

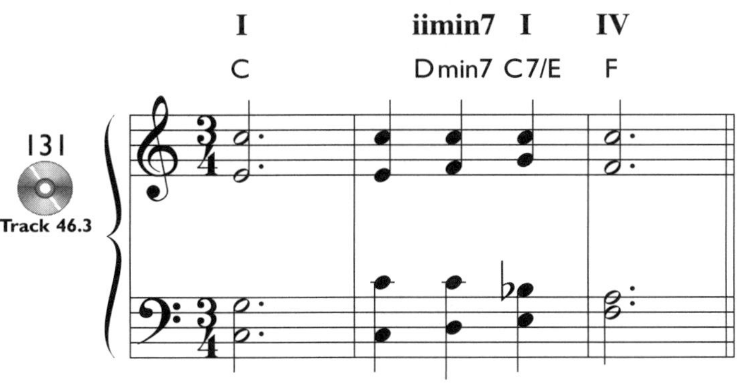

The vamp, built on a repeated phrase in the chorus (usually just two chords to facilitate improvisation, although sometimes more) shows up in a high percentage of Gospel compositions. This is the place where vocalists exhibit their highest degree of artistry and where choir and congregation are in the heights of religious fervor. The vamp may be longer than the rest of the tune several times over. The close of the vamp is often signaled by some variation of the choral phrase or a preset phrase from the soloist. Endings often include virtuoso cadenza displays from the soloist, and, if audience enthusiasm warrants, some portion of the vamp and the final cadence are likely to be reprised.

CHAPTER 12

Jazz and Fusion Blues

All serious jazz players acknowledge the importance of the blues and most consider themselves to be blues players. However, when saying they "play the blues," they mean they use the twelve-bar blues form with sophisticated changes, usually in the key of F, as a framework for virtuosic improvisation. The vocabulary of the blues is present in the playing of a high percentage of jazz artists and serves as a counterbalance against a level of complexity that would lose touch with the average listener, a tendency that is recurrent in jazz. In this method, we have already mentioned many pianists who had credible reputations as both jazz and blues pianists.

Twentieth-century jazz can be roughly divided into four chronological styles/eras using major artists as references:

1. **Traditional Jazz** (Ragtime, Dixieland through Big Band Swing): Scott Joplin, Edward Kennedy "Duke" Ellington, William "Count" Basie and a host of other big band pianists, along with Fats Waller, Jelly Roll Morton, Art Tatum, Oscar Peterson and their peers.

2. **Bop and Post Bop:** Charlie Parker, Dizzy Gillespie, Charles Mingus; pianists Bud Powell, Thelonius Monk, Lenny Tristano, Tommy Flanagan, McCoy Tyner and others too numerous to mention.

3. **Cool and Modal Jazz**: Miles Davis in his middle years, pianists Bill Evans, Horace Silver, Red Garland, Wynton Kelly, Herbie Hancock ... the list goes on.

4. **Jazz Rock/Fusion**: Miles Davis again, post "Bitches Brew" and "Live Evil" with keyboard players Herbie Hancock (again—a major figure), Keith Jarrett, Joseph Zawinul, Chick Corea and a host of others.

The popularity of traditional jazz continues to the present day, as does that of hard bop. Post bop, as typified by John Coltrane, branched off into free jazz—the so called "New Thing"—in the early and middle 1960s. This was "reaction music" utilizing the skills of the bop school. The influence of the modal period is still evident in "smooth jazz" and the atmospheric waftings of New Age mood music. However, smooth jazz is actually the disowned step-child of the fusion movement, and fusion itself has been disowned by many proponents of the other styles.

What all these different styles share, and what distinguishes them from mainstream blues, is the playing of changes—finding an appropriate scale for each chord (whatever its duration). In mainstream blues, we usually play from a parent scale (usually some form of the blues scale) over a group of related chord changes. In this chapter, we'll take a look at information and concepts that go along with playing changes.

NATURAL MODES AND SYNTHETIC SCALES

The first place to look for a scale to fit a given chord is the twelve major key signatures, each of which contains seven natural modes. The modes are listed below with the Greek names customarily assigned to them and the chords (with all extensions), that they can be used over.

IONIAN (SAME AS THE MAJOR SCALE)

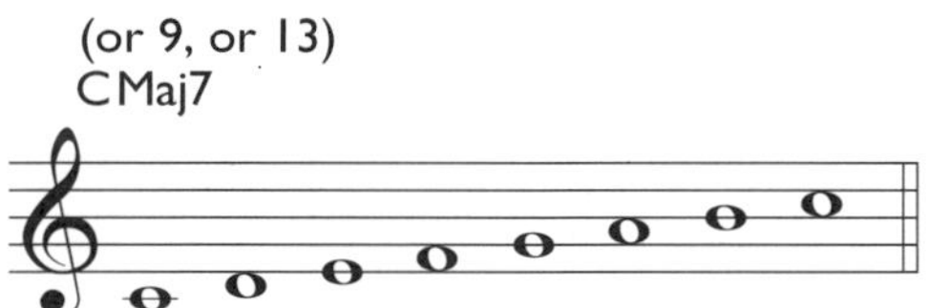

DORIAN

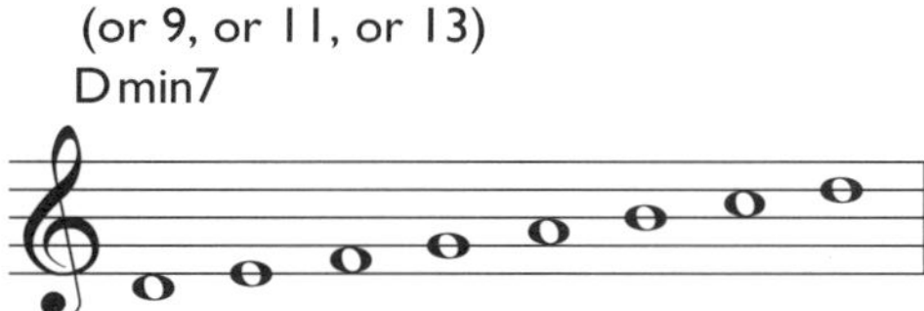

PHRYGIAN

LYDIAN

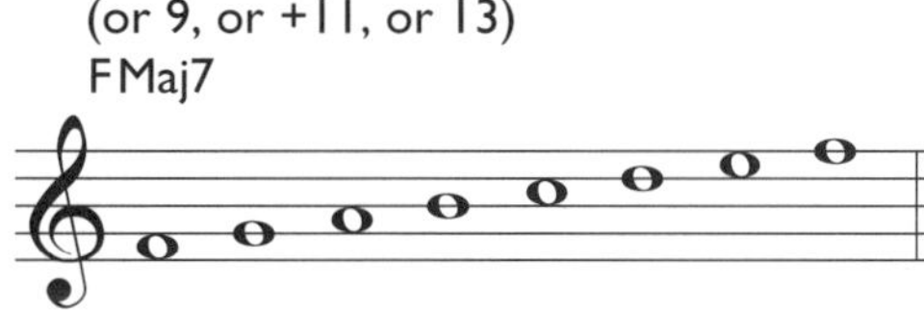

MIXOLYDIAN

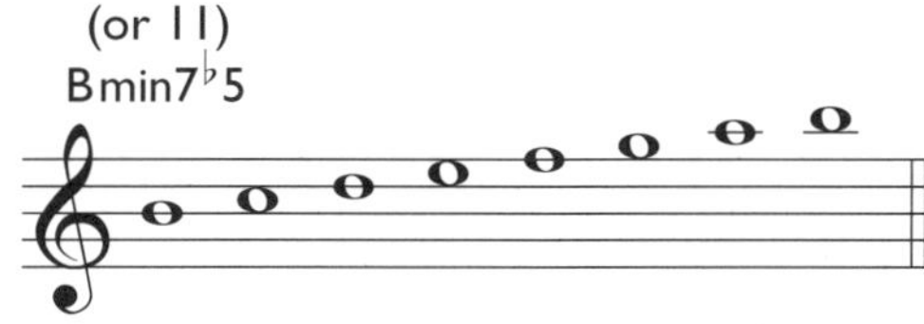

AEOLIAN (SAME AS THE NATURAL MINOR SCALE)

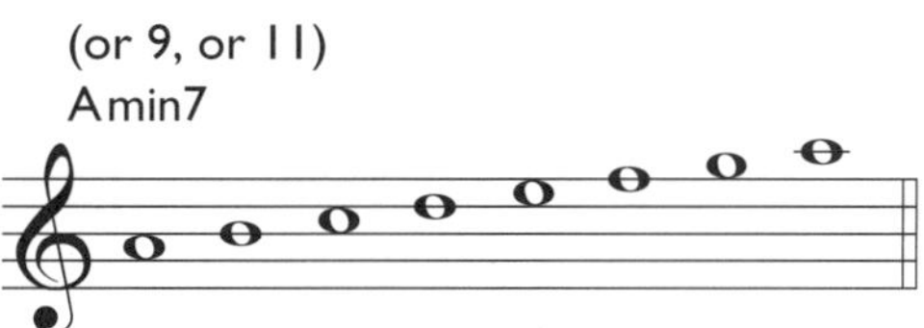

LOCRIAN

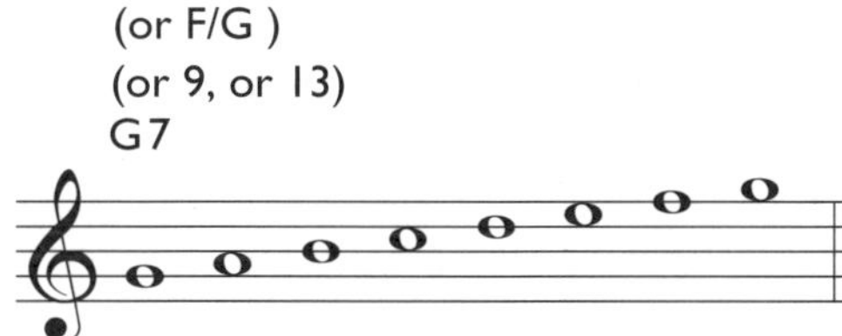

Play each scale over the 7th chord indicated in all keys. As you do this, see if you can feel the resolution tendency of each half step. Each mode has its own unique flavor and extra-musical associations. Ionian and Aeolian are the familiar major and minor, Dorian is characterized as "heroic," although it has associations with Celtic folk melodies as well. Phrygian clearly says "Spanish." Lydian is generally delicate and otherworldly, while Mixolydian, with its flatted 7th degree, has an earthy connection to the blues. The Locrian mode is infrequently used in a modal way. Rather, it is more often found in the context of a chord progression. It suggests the grotesque and misshapen. Become familiar with them all!

Make sure that you are fluent with the modes in all keys. This is not terribly difficult—if you have a secure knowledge of key signatures, and memorize which degree of the major scale is the root of each mode, it is not a great leap to play in any chosen mode in any key. Try all the modes shown above in all keys. You should also determine the whole-step/half-step structure of each mode and memorize them. For example, practice playing all seven modes from the same root (C Ionian, C Dorian, C Phrygian, etc.).

In this book, everything should be played with a swing feel unless marked "*Straight 8ths.*"

The recommended tempo for all the examples on this page is ♩ = 120.

PLAYING CHANGES

Having established the scale for each chord in a given chord progression, the next step in learning to improvise in a jazz style is to practice running motifs through the changes. Here is an example of a simple motif over a turnaround:

Begin to collect motifs for jazz playing. You will need many. Keep them in your notebook. Remember the "Golden Rule of Repetition" (see page 19): do not use a single pattern more than three times without alteration, except when practicing.

EXTENSIONS AND ALTERED EXTENSIONS

Jazz differs from blues in that more extended harmonies are used. When voicing extensions in the left hand, the 9th can replace the root and the 11th and/or 13th can replace the 5th. Altering the extension can heighten the tension this creates—9ths can be sharped or flatted, 11ths can be augmented and 13ths flatted (a flatted 13th implies that a 5th is present in the chord, otherwise it would sound the same as an augmented 5th). Example 134 shows some common extended chords as they would be voiced in the right hand, without roots or 5ths.

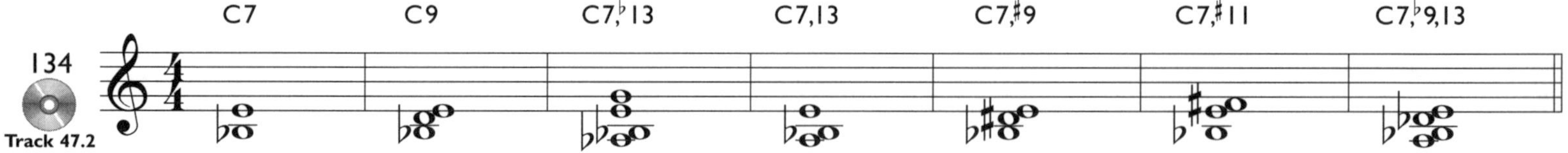

Scales must be altered to fit these altered extensions. Here, the F is sharped to conform to the altered 11th.

In this example, the D and A are flatted to conform to the altered 9th and 13th, respectively.

These two choruses use a handful of motifs in a mainstream-jazz style. They illustrate playing the changes. Notice how a passage in the blues scale (the last two bars) brings the solo back down to earth. Keep the left hand simple so that you can focus on how the lines work with the harmonies.

THE BLUES CHANGES EVERYTHING

Track 48

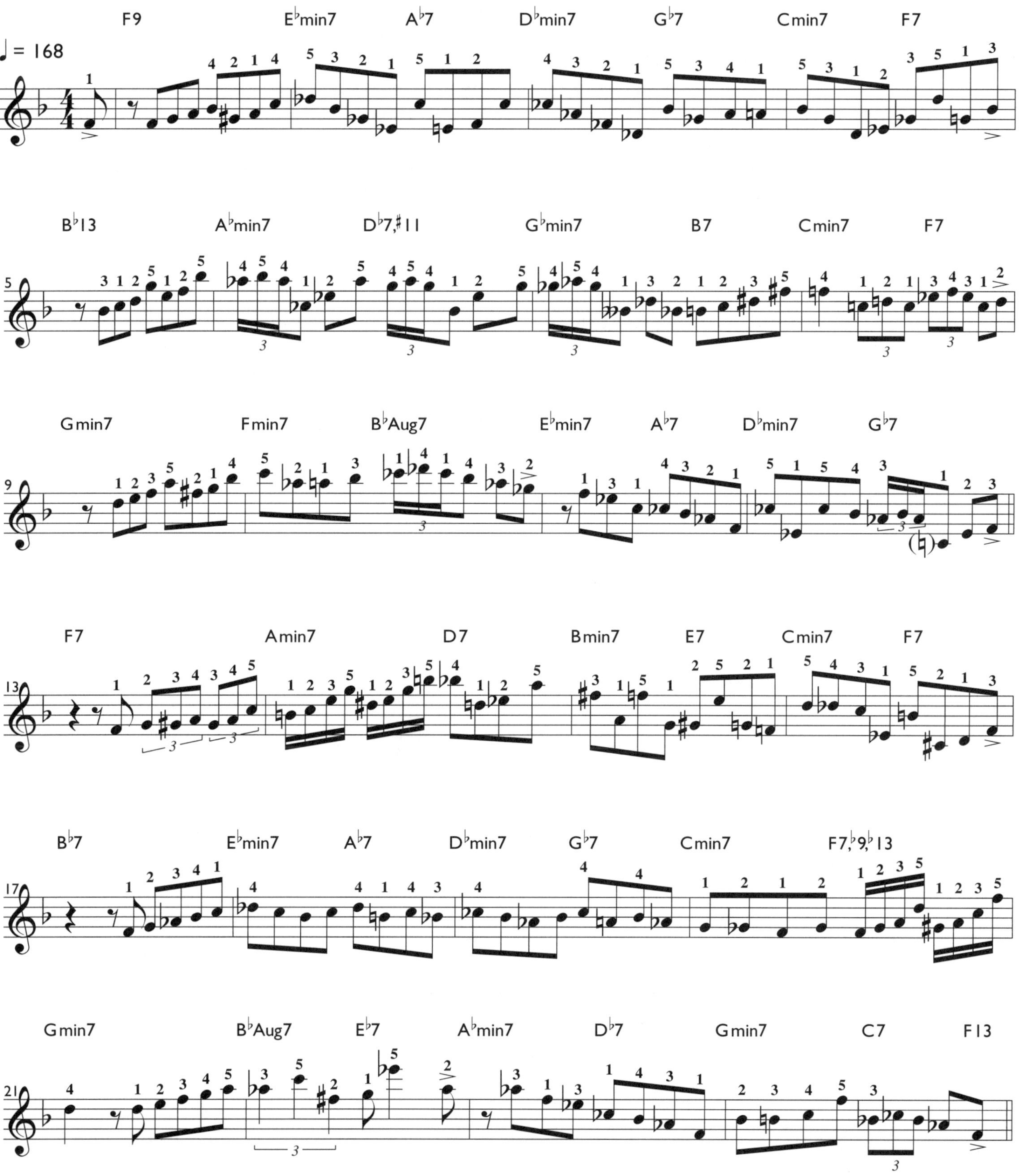

EXPANDING THE PARAMETERS

Beginning in the 1960s, jazz was radically transformed by the fusion movement. The "third stream" experiments of the 1950s, combining jazz with European classical music, were followed by experiments with Indian classical music, Arabic, Balinese, Japanese, Celtic, traditional African music from all parts of that continent and the contemporary European "avante garde." "World music" collaborations and unusual instrumentations thrived. People like Dave Brubeck, Don Ellis, Miles Davis and John McLaughlin's Mahavishnu Orchestra played the blues in odd meters. The use of space, pioneered by Basie and Monk, became cosmic in the recordings of Miles Davis. There were experiments with playing in two simultaneous meters. Indian rhythmic structures and scales and European *twelve-tone rows* (a modern classical compositional technique) occasionally found their way into blues compositions. The harmonic vocabulary, already having adopted the harmonic innovations of the French impressionists (chord extensions), expanded to include other techniques such as *polytonality* (playing in more than one key simultaneously). Players sometimes superimposed melodies or improvised lines with new key centers over the blues progression, and borrowings were made from the more extreme harmonic and formal experimentation of Igor Stravinsky, Bela Bartok, Edgar Varese, Olivier Messiaen and Karlheinz Stockhausen.

A telling example of the limits to which the blues have been stretched is *Celestial Terrestrial Commuters* on *The Mahavishnu Orchestra's* "Birds of Fire" LP. The band members improvised freely over an eleven-bar form in $\frac{19}{16}$ ($\frac{6}{8}$ + $\frac{6}{16}$ separated by a single sixteenth note.) The subdominant is replaced by the II chord in bar 4 and by the ♭iii chord in bar 9. The dominant is replaced by the ♭V chord. The scale of the ostinato which the tune is built on is transposed to each of these scale degrees. It is a major scale with a raised 4th degree and a lowered 7th degree. The melody uses this scale, also, but mixes in substantial material from the familiar blues scale. The soloists all regroup the subdivisions within each bar and always come out on the downbeat. All this at the rapid pace of over 400 sixteenth notes per minute! This was a stunning display of musicianship and compositional skill from an unearthly realm, yet it is still easily recognizable as the blues.

In the following composition you may be able to identify some of these devices. Notice that each measure of 22 eighth notes is divided into three sub-measures ($\frac{5}{4}$, $\frac{6}{8}$ and $\frac{6}{8}$) marked with dotted bar lines. Count "1 & 2 & 3 & 4 & 5 &, 1 2 3 4 5 6, 1 2 3 4 5 6" keeping the speed of the eighth notes steady. Have fun!

Cmin
Gmin
pp
F/E♭
E♭/D♭
Dmin
E♭/D
Dmin7
Amin7
B♭/A
To Coda
B
A♭dim
Play 3 times
2nd time solo
3rd time as written
Play 3 times
A♭ Lydian
rit.
tr
8va
D.S. al Coda
Coda
Gmin
(White key glisses)

INTO THE FUTURE

Congratulations on having completed
Mastering Blues Keyboard* and *The Complete Blues Keyboard Method.

Traditionally, becoming a blues player meant becoming a sideman with an established artist for a number of years. If such an opportunity presents itself, jump on it! In the meantime, play every chance you get with players better than yourself to improve your skills. Teach players less proficient than you are, not only to solidify your own understanding and performance but also to continue, on some level, the verbal transmission of knowledge which is traditional in the blues.

Until recent years, the bandstand was the only blues school. Recording technology breakthroughs, specifically CD players that can advance through a tune one note at a time and also slow a tune without changing its pitch, have made transcription and rote memorization possible—even for musicians with only modest ear training. There are also numerous published collections of keyboard solos from prominent artists. The technology and methods such as this however, cannot completely replace the mentor/apprentice relationship.

At the very least, it is hoped this method has given you a glimpse into the vastness of the blues and given you an appreciation for the geniuses who originated and developed the music. It is also hoped that you have gained a sense of certainty that the blues will endure. Whatever devices we may use to make our music, the unbroken thread of the blues will always be there to remind us of who we are and where we have been; it will continue to humanize our music and our lives.

DISCOGRAPHY

Atlantic Blues	Four-CD set including blues piano compilation with Jimmy Yancey, Professor Longhair, Meade Lux Lewis, etc. There is also great piano playing on the vocal and guitar compilations. (Atlantic Records)
Blues by Roosevelt Sykes	Roosevelt Sykes. (Smithsonian Folkways)
Blues Essentials	Compilation with Muddy Waters, Elmore James, Memphis Slim, Howlin Wolf, etc. (Capitol Records)
Birth of Soul	Ray Charles. (Atlantic Records)
Boogie Woogie, Stride and Piano Blues	With Pete Johnson, James P. Johnson, etc. (EMI Records)
Dr. John Plays Mac Rebbenack	Dr. John. (Rounder Records) Solo piano. (Clean Cuts Records)
Essential Blues Piano	Great blues piano compilation with Otis Spann, Lafayette Leake, Pinetop Perkins, Katie Webster, etc. (House of Blues)
Hoochie Coochie Man/ Got My Mojo Workin'	Jimmy Smith. (Verve Records)
Jump Back Honey	Hadda Brooks. The complete OKeh sessions. (Columbia)
Live and Well *Live at the Regal*	B.B. King. (MCA Records)
New Orleans Piano	Professor Longhair. (Atlantic)
Memphis Slim	Memphis Slim. (Chess MCA Records)
Patriarch of the Blues	Sunnyland Slim. (Opal Records)
Rekooperation	Al Kooper. (BMG Music)
Spiders on the Keys	James Booker. (Rounder)
Texas Flood	Stevie Ray Vaughan. (Epic records). Classic example of modern blues guitar.
The Blues Never Die	Otis Spann. (Prestige Records)
The Chess 50th Anniversary Collection	Muddy Waters. (Chess/MCA Records)
The Complete Recordings	Robert Johnson. No keyboards here, but he may be the most important blues artist ever. (Columbia Records)
Vocal Accompaniment and Early Post-war Recordings: 1930-1954	Little Brother Montgomery. (Document Records)

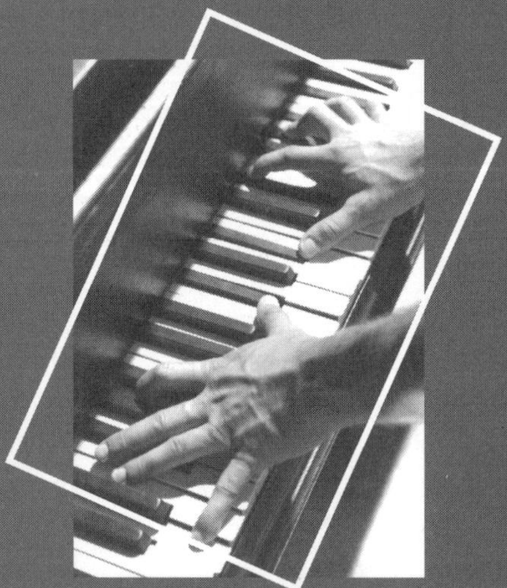